The New Enlightenment

David Graham was born in Taunton, Somerset, and educated at the universities of Bristol and Indiana. He joined the BBC in 1970 and later became producer of the Nationwide Consumer Unit. He was deputy editor of *The Money Programme* and from 1979–82 was a producer on *Panorama*. He worked on the Channel Four Steering Committee and, with Peter Donebauer, founded Diverse Production Ltd to produce programmes for Channel Four. It is now one of Britain's most prolific 'independents' and has made almost two hundred programmes for Channel Four. David Graham is executive producer of *Diverse Reports*, and is managing director responsible for programme production and development.

Peter Clarke was born in Venice and educated in Scotland, Barrow and Loughborough. He graduated from Bradford University and studied economics at Balliol College, Oxford. After teaching economics at the Conservative staff college at Swindon and a spell as an economist in industry, he worked as a broadcaster for LBC and as an economics correspondent for the BBC. Since 1984 he has contributed to Channel Four's *Diverse Reports*. He has been chairman of the Selsdon Group, is now director of the David Hume Institute in Edinburgh and is a freelance journalist. He has recently been selected as a Conservative candidate for East Lothian.

The New Enlightenment

the rebirth of liberalism

David Graham
and Peter Clarke

MACMILLAN
LONDON

in association with Channel Four Television Company Limited

This book is based on the television series,
The New Enlightenment, produced for Channel Four Television by Diverse Production Limited.

First published 1986 by
MACMILLAN LONDON LIMITED
4 Little Essex Street London WC2R 3LF
and Basingstoke

Associated companies in Auckland, Delhi, Dublin, Gaborone, Hamburg, Harare, Hong Kong, Johannesburg, Kuala Lumpur, Lagos, Manzini, Melbourne, Mexico City, Nairobi, New York, Singapore and Tokyo

British Library Cataloguing in Publication Data

Graham, David and Clarke, Peter
The new enlightenment: the rebirth of liberalism
1. Political science
I. Title
320'.01 JA66

ISBN 0-333-43494-3

Typeset by Rowland Phototypesetting Limited
Bury St Edmunds, Suffolk, and London
Printed in Great Britain by
Camelot Press Limited, Southampton

Contents

Acknowledgements

As this book is part of a television project, its debts are numerous. The series, *The New Enlightenment*, was produced by Diverse Production Ltd, London. We would like to thank Liz Forgan, Deputy Controller of Programmes and Senior Commissioning Editor for News and Current Affairs at Channel 4, for supporting and encouraging the series. The video crew who filmed the series around the world were Sean Leslie, Paul Nathan and Simon Sharkey. Pippa Robinson was the production assistant, and we had assistance from April Oliver in New York. The producer, Philip Clarke, has made an enormous contribution to the development of the idea, and helped greatly with the writing of this book, as did our two researchers. We thank Matthew Hoffman for his invaluable work in the United States and for a major contribution to the series, and Jeremy Bristow for his work on Japan, Switzerland and the British National Health Service. The Reason Foundation of Santa Monica helped to raise funds for the project.

We owe special thanks to Robert Poole of the Reason Foundation for his support in the early days and to Lynn Scarlett for a very special brand of help. We must also thank Chris Tame, for preliminary research on the project, and our colleague Anna Coote, who came up with the idea, though we will not expect her to agree with our conclusions. The book was written at enormous speed. We have to thank Richard Bunning and Ian Harries at Diverse Production for setting up the Wordstar system to handle the book, Rik Bryant for extra keystroking, Gillian Faulkner for expertly keeping the world turning while we were away, and Peter Donebauer for taking over his partner's business responsibilities.

An enormous number of people gave us advice. Those who were interviewed are listed at the beginning of each chapter. We also have to thank Antony Fisher for helping us to get support for the series, and the Institute of Economic Affairs in London for continuous help and interest. Lord Harris of High Cross and Arthur Seldon read parts of the manuscript. Matthew Hoffman checked it. The biggest debt we owe is to the old battler, Frederick Hayek, who saw us more often than he should have done and to whom we are all deeply grateful.

Introduction

This book is part of a project for television. It shares to some extent the character of its parent medium. Television is not a good vehicle for ideas. It is documentary. It is interested in stories, in people, in the reasons people do the things they do. It loves big public events and international scope. It is not scholarly.

All of that makes us poor candidates to conduct a dispassionate survey of the leading ideas within what we call the 'New Enlightenment'. But such surveys have been written, and you should read one. Better still, go and get one of the key volumes, Nozick's *Anarchy, State, and Utopia* or Hayek's *The Constitution of Liberty*.

This book does a different job. These six essays are openly polemical, subjective, non-exhaustive and 'committed'. Indeed, the book is written for a specific group of people. It is written for busy people who, in their daily perception of what is happening around them, are beginning to feel root assumptions being shaken. If so, they are probably a bit like us.

Most of the people working on this project have been making television programmes on public issues for some years. In Britain, the 1970s were a depressing and disturbing time to report on. Most television producers were, and still are, on the left. They are socialists or social democrats. In Britain, they work in a public service. That was true of us, too.

Then, in different ways, minds were changed, usually as a result of particular experiences. This is how it happened to me. As unemployment rose at the end of the 1970s, I started to make a programme about the long-term adult unemployed and spent six weeks observing a place of deepest poverty in Scotland. It was a council estate of 500 people. I shall simply call it The Scheme.

The homes of The Scheme were grey apartment blocks.

Individual flats were derelict, some buildings abandoned. The Scheme was surrounded by old mine workings, long dead, and steelworks now dying too. The old ironworks was in the last stages of demolition, only its blast furnace still standing; another mill was waiting to be broken up, and the rolling mill was laying men off. Nearby, there was a domestic appliance factory, which employed many women, and a chicken-packing company. In the distance you could see the cranes along the Clyde, standing up like sentries, waiting for ships.

I had the trust of families living on The Scheme. My card had been marked by a well-known man on the left, the convenor of a Clydeside shipyard, who lived not far away. I got to know people well, and I do not believe there was much they were afraid to tell.

When a man lost his job, he would start, full of contempt for other 'idle' people, convinced he would resume work right away. That almost never happened. There were then three ways he might go. He might become a determined job-seeker, and keep on looking, sometimes for years, willing to work sometimes for even less than he got on the 'broo'. Such men usually found work one day. They were a small minority. A second group became discouraged quickly, and settled for a domestic routine of cooking, decorating, a little gardening, going for the 'messages' in the mornings. They were the saddest group.

The other unemployed men, just under a half of the total, it seemed to me, did various kinds of illegal undeclared work. Some prepared cars for MOT tests (there were places in their homes where neat toolsets were covertly stored). Others collected scrap or extracted lead from old appliances, trading it locally. One successful man had learned photography and specialised in wedding photographs and albums. His house stood out. The garden was bright and the lawn mown. None of these activities amounted to a living. Families were then receiving between £50 and £90 per week depending on size: the supplementary activities might add £10 or £15. People enjoyed talking about their undeclared work. It was exciting and it gave them pleasure. There was, however, an informal rule that no one should be too 'greedy'; if someone was, a neighbour would lift a phone.

What united the men and women was their total contempt for the 'system', especially the poverty trap, that absurd disincentive for work that followed from the way benefits are assessed. 'We didn't invent the system,' they would say, always anticipating blame. They knew that the heroes of the world outside The Scheme were the determined job-seekers, even if it meant working for less than what they could take home on the dole. The situation was most absurd for the wives of the unemployed. Because of the rule that a woman's declared earnings could only add £2 to the dole money, women quit work when their husbands lost their jobs, even though there were jobs for women in the area. The happiest group was those who did undeclared work.

We broadcast all this and a little of the underground economy of undeclared work, though it was difficult to film. The reaction was interesting. On the left, the film was condemned. At TV seminars it was shown and criticised as a form of implicit propaganda. Revealing the 'black economy' was part of a design to discredit the welfare system and show up 'scroungers', it was said. Apparently, the correct, compassionate thing to do was not to talk about the problem or to consider reforms of the social security system.

There were no complaints from Scotland, since the film was true. But the opposition clarified my thoughts, made me think about myself. I was pretty sure that if I had to live on The Scheme I would do illegal, undeclared work. It was the only option which possessed any dignity. The plight of the determined job-seeker was awful, turning up daily at the same factory gate or vacancy board. The do-nothings were sad beyond belief. Only the illicit workers were enjoying what they did. It was still a rotten life, but they were doing something with it. What is more, though no one seemed willing to admit it, they were doing something useful. Raising scrap or saving lead or taking photographs are useful things to do.

The problem of The Scheme was immobility. No one could go anywhere or leave the one place in Scotland where they were entitled to a council house. All over the country the poor were locked into poverty. And the physical immobility of the men and women of The Scheme was a mere emblem of the immobility imposed by the welfare system. The left was refusing to acknowledge the problem. It might speak of 'industrial regeneration'. One look at Clydeside told you that the world's ships would not be back.

That sent me off to look for other ideas, and took me down a road along which, one by one, assumptions were abandoned, friends lost and others gained. My world changed. Six years after I went to Scotland, I know that the men on The Scheme had that essential creative spirit which we call entrepreneurship. Now I have been lucky enough, with others, to be able to explore the liberal revival all over the world and speak to its best minds. There is nothing comprehensive about our journey. In Japan, in India, in America, in Switzerland, in Italy and, yes, occasionally, in Britain we just try to capture events and people that tell something hopeful, something promising, something new. Our excitement has never wavered. We have never doubted, not for a minute, that we are looking at the greatest political shift of our century.

David Graham
London, July 1986

1
The Death of Socialism

The major political event of the twentieth century is the death of socialism.

Irving Kristol, in conversation

History often reflects the tensions between philosophies. One such philosophy called socialism is falling apart. A new one is taking its place. We do not know exactly what to call it, so we have described it as the revival of classical liberalism. This book relates what we think is *the* political story of our time. It is about ideas, pursued not in the calm of the study, but through the flux of political events, influenced as they are by personality and coincidence. The book makes no claim to be complete.

This first chapter looks at the past and takes us to the present.

The imaginations of the West in the hundred years from 1850 were captured by socialism and science. Intellectuals were dazzled by the triumphs of theoretical and applied science and they began to believe that human affairs could be studied and ordered in a scientific fashion. The works of Karl Marx, of John Maynard Keynes, even of Sigmund Freud, were ingenious attempts to match the accomplishments of physics, biology and engineering.

The new philosophy turns another way. It explores what is created by spontaneous, uncoordinated action. It claims that the real mysteries of human achievement are exactly those that no one ever intended to design. Language, music and law, for example, evolve without conscious plan. Each great writer or jurist labours to expand the range of a medium, but each inherits systems which are the products of millions of

The writing of this chapter has been greatly helped by conversations with Paul Johnson, John Gray, Martin Anderson, Lord Harris of High Cross, Antony Fisher, Milton Friedman and Frederick Hayek.[1]

other unplanned contributions. People who put their faith in the organising power of one person's reason are making the same mistake as Dr Samuel Johnson, who thought that the English language would stop growing and changing after publication of his dictionary. We are blessed with systems which let us do vast and complicated things together or for one another. As Kenneth Minogue has it, we are like 'baboons seated at a giant Wurlitzer organ'.[2] 'Catallaxy' was the word the Greeks used for the orders which men can create 'which are the result of action, not design'. The New Enlightenment has rediscovered the idea. In this book we try to explain how individuals, by their independent actions, are a greater force for good than the most ingenious blueprint for social organisation.

Another word which we shall be using a lot is 'market': in a market, a small sign called a 'price' co-ordinates the actions of thousands of people and brings together, out of the throng of humanity, strangers with something useful to exchange.

There are some other terms we need to clarify. When we use the word 'liberal' we use it in what we think is its correct meaning. In fact, that is the last time it will appear between inverted commas when used in this chosen sense. In future, we will only place 'liberal' between inverted commas when we use it in a corrupted sense. We think liberal describes the view that humans are rational beings who should be left, as far as possible, to pursue their own purposes without compulsion or constraint. The word first appears in the English language in the fourteenth century and refers to free men as distinct from those who are not free. That meaning has shifted. Particularly in America, 'liberal' has come to denote the idea that a person's primary role is his membership of a group. It is a synonym for 'progressive' or 'radical'. Thus 'liberal' is associated with intervention in the economy and with an extensive redistribution of wealth. The word probably acquired this meaning at the time of Franklin Roosevelt's New Deal and reached its meridian at the time of Lyndon Johnson's Great Society. This was a period when many Americans looked to the state to provide them with both a prosperous and a 'moral' society. In Europe the use of a regulated free-enterprise system to enable politicians to achieve social objectives and a 'fair' distribution of wealth is called 'social democracy' or 'socialism'. We shall usually call it 'socialism'. It is important to note that the Liberal Party of Great Britain has only a tenuous connection with the ideas in this book.

We have called this book *The New Enlightenment* because the movement we describe is a lineal descendant of the Scottish Enlightenment which flourished in the eighteenth century. In the Scottish Enlightenment the concepts of individual liberty developed by the English philosopher John Locke were joined with the free-market ideas of the Edinburgh circle of Adam Smith, whose *The Wealth of Nations* was published in 1776. This tradition leads directly to the American Revolution, to the American Constitution of 1787, and to the Bill of Rights in 1791.

What marks this tradition is its commitment to individual liberty. The Enlightenment in Britain marked the establishment of a commercial society in which a freely negotiated contract replaced the master–servant order as the model of social relationships. It was not a revolutionary movement. This Scottish Enlightenment was informed by a gentle, self-limiting scepticism. It firmly acknowledged the limits of reason. On the Continent of Europe a very different Enlightenment took place, which, born in more conservative and structured societies, fostered the belief that reason would remake the world. Its objectives were much more ambitious. It was rationalist and dirigiste. It culminated in a French Revolution that, in its impatience to overthrow restrictive traditional forms, took away all impediments to tyranny. This French Enlightenment leads to Marxism and socialism.

The Scottish Enlightenment picked up a particularly Anglo-Saxon kind of individualism and worked it into a system of thought that combines two tendencies. Adam Ferguson, Adam Smith and David Hume were interested in human psychology. That gave them a knowledge of human failings and made them modest about what men, individually or collectively, can comprehend or design. On the other hand they were expansive about the amount of wealth creation which systems reflecting a modest and limiting view of the human condition can bring about.

The two styles of Enlightenment were given historical form in the two very different revolutions of France and America. As Rousseau was the inspiration of the movement to overthrow the French monarchy, so John Locke was the inspiration of the colonial movement to be rid of the British Crown. The tradition we are reporting on is therefore an Anglo-American tradition, which has some roots in other places and is now spreading across the world. As everyone must know, the governments of Margaret Thatcher and Ronald Reagan are influenced by these ideas. We will explain how that happened.

Some will feel that *The New Enlightenment* is a grandiose title which claims too much. It is true that New Enlightenment thinkers do not believe that the future is predictable. It is also true that only the future will tell if true enlightenment has taken place. Nevertheless, with those two cautions in mind, we press on, impelled by the belief that the movement holds immense potential for change and that what we are describing is a paradigm shift. This notion of a 'paradigm' was developed by the philosopher of science Thomas Kuhn.[3] He argued that all 'normal science' takes place within a certain theoretical framework or view of the world. As scientists explore reality or as history provides new events to scrutinise, we discover bits that do not fit in with this world view. Being basically conservative, we work hard to defend our theories against these anomalies and so stay within our existing paradigms. (For example, Karl Marx said that workers would be impoverished by capitalism. They were not. So Marxists invented new forms of 'spiritual impoverishment' to keep the theory alive.) Eventually, a 'scientific revolution' occurs. Someone proposes a new theory – one that explains the anomalies which troubled its predecessors. If the theory is accepted, it becomes a new paradigm.

The major players in the New Enlightenment are modest and cautious about their work. Their methods are tentative. They seek contradiction as much as verification. They share the view that progress is random and capricious and incapable of exact prediction. They redefine scientific progress as something haphazard and accidental. They believe, profoundly, in the law of unintended consequences which says that in all our projects we invariably achieve something different from what we foresaw when we embarked on them. Nevertheless, optimism lights their ideas. The future, according to Frederick Hayek, the leading activist of this intellectual movement, 'feels hopeful'.[4] In the sunlit uplands of that possible future, they see freedom supported by prosperity, regulated by modest and sensible laws. Can we unlock the paradox in which modesty and confidence coexist? The key to the puzzle is the idea of spontaneous order.

Hayek finds this idea in Roman law, in the pre-Socratic philosophers and, unexpectedly, in one Dr Bernard Mandeville, an eccentric whose work *The Fable of the Bees* (1714) was a *succès de scandale* in England over 250 years ago.[5] He achieved notoriety with such lines as:

> The worst of all the multitude
> Did something for the common good.

Mandeville, who came originally from Holland, was by profession a doctor who specialised in mental cases, a sort of early psychiatrist. That may have given him a realistic view of human motivation. Mandeville's *Fable of the Bees* described a hive of egoistic creatures who could, in spite of their selfishness, combine together to form a rich and even happy community. This doggerel poem inspired Mandeville to develop the theme that, even if individual actions were selfish and malevolent, the results could be rational and beneficent. A more level statement of the idea comes in *The Wealth of Nations* (1776):

> every individual necessarily labours to render the annual revenue of the society as great as he can. He generally, indeed, neither intends to promote the public interest, nor knows how much he is promoting it. . . . he intends only his own gain, and he is in this, as in many other cases, led by an invisible hand to promote an end which is no part of his intention.[6]

The intellectual exploration of this idea has been one of the great adventures of the last two centuries.

Hayek celebrates Mandeville as a man struggling towards a theory of the spontaneous growth of orderly social structures. Hayek's great importance is that he has thoroughly remodelled this idea for our time, and defended it with enormous energy. The theory holds that the complex order of society that results from men's actions is quite different from what they had intended. It says that individuals, in pursuing their own ends, whether selfish or altruistic, usually produce results that are good for others, though they do not anticipate this and may not even know about it. This is because their actions are guided to these useful ends by institutions, customs and rules which were never deliberately invented but which have survived and developed because they were found successful. The order of society, even what we call culture, is the result of individual strivings with no such orderly end in view. The evolution of rules and customs is like that of animal species, selecting and preserving what works best.

Frederick Hayek was born in Vienna on 8 May 1899 into a scholarly family. As a young man he could not make up his mind whether to be an economist or a psychologist. At that time he held mild Fabian socialist opinions which a visit to the United States as a research student did nothing to change. He was weaned from his socialism by the great economist of the 'Austrian' school, Ludwig von Mises, who gave him his first job even though Hayek had skipped Mises' lectures at university. At discussion groups in Mises' office he began to understand the problems of socialism and became a convert when he read Mises' critique, *Socialism*, in 1922. For the rest of his life he explored the truths of the Austrian school.

The Austrian school sees society as a complex of human interactions, in which prices act as signals for human behaviour. By contrast, a socialist society that sees human beings as raw material waiting to be shaped by government is likely to prove nasty, brutish and short on economic success. For the Austrian economist the free market and the language of price are the very sources and mechanisms of wealth. The diversity of goods produced by many individuals is richer and more useful, ensuring greater and more widespread wealth than any system which attempts to control from the centre. A diversity of different attempts to predict future needs is what guarantees innovation. The role of market pricing is partly that of allocating resources to the preferred use. Its more important role, however, is that of transmitting information about preferences and about relative scarcities. Only markets can effectively utilise information dispersed throughout the society among literally millions of economic agents. Profit is the signal which demonstrates that the entrepreneur is doing the right thing for people he cannot possibly know. Price is therefore the language of the complex or extended order of modern societies. The knowledge utilised in this extended order is greater than that which any single agent such as a government department can possibly acquire.

If Frederick Hayek is the leading activist of the New Enlightenment, Karl Popper is its presiding spirit. Popper, too, was raised in Vienna. As a young man he absorbed Marx's theory of history, Freud's psychoanalysis and the so-called 'individual psychology' of Alfred Adler. What impressed Popper and his young friends in post-war Austria was the extraordinary explanatory power of these theories. 'Once your eyes were opened you saw confirming instances everywhere,' he says. The theories had the character of 'revelations'.[7]

Alfred Adler was famous as the inventor of the theory of the 'inferiority complex'. This maintains that all human beings have profound feelings of inferiority which they acquire from their experience as totally helpless infants. In later life, they learn to 'compensate' for this, particularly in their family lives. If they fail to do this satisfactorily they may be led into neurotic behaviour. One day Popper, who knew Adler personally, brought him a case which he just could not fit into this scheme of things. But Adler found no difficulty, analysing the case in terms of his own theory of the inferiority complex without even seeing the patient. Popper asked him how he could be so sure. 'Because of my thousandfold experience,' Adler replied. Popper found the answer infuriating and later realised why. Adler's was a 'heads I win, tails you lose' kind of theory.

In the same year, 1919, another theory was being tested: Einstein's theory of relativity. Popper knew that it would be confirmed if Eddington's observation of the 1919 eclipse achieved exactly the results predicted. Popper's small circle were thrilled when the right results came in. Popper himself was then struck by the contrast between the two cases. Einstein's theory could be observed and tested. But there was a definite risk in this procedure. Einstein's theory laid itself open to refutation if the predicted effect did not occur. Adler's theory, however, like Marx's theory of history, took no risks. It was irrefutable. It could never be tested. It could shift, jelly-like, before any new fact. Popper concluded that there was no way of knowing whether these no-risk theories were true. Therefore they did not help us much to understand reality. They certainly were not 'scientific' theories.

From then on Popper concentrated on the theory of scientific knowledge, and spent a lifetime revising our understanding of how we acquire it. He showed that the assumption that we proceed to a hypothesis from empirical observation is wrong. He used to demonstrate this by asking his students to 'observe'. They did not know what to do or where to start. In this way he showed that observation must be focused by a guess or hypothesis, which it should then be designed to confirm or refute. A scientific discovery is more likely to be an inspired guess which you then test than the product of long observation. So Popper puts inspiration and creativity, rather than observation, in the first phase of scientific discovery. But his work contains an implicit warning. Most knowledge is, as the Ancient Greek Xenophanes put it, 'but a woven web of guesses'.[8]

This spirit informs the New Enlightenment. Its basic ideas are simple. Its theories have caution in their bones. They would not have become part of a political movement had it not been for the appalling history of our times.

The great evil of our century, according to Paul Johnson's book, *The History of the Modern World* (1982), has been the rise in the power of the state and the arrival of totalitarianism.[9] This has occurred alongside a collapse of the Judaeo-Christian notion of personal responsibility. That collapse was engineered in different ways by Karl Marx and Sigmund Freud. Individuals became flotsam, driven here and there by irresistible forces, economic or psychic or whatever. In the name of Marx's 'inevitable laws', whole races and classes have been subjugated or liquidated. In the century of what Paul Johnson calls the 'despotic utopia', the state has burgeoned, expanding above all in destructive power. 'War socialism' has vastly increased the size of the state in democracies, bringing into public life new kinds of political figures: career politicians and career civil servants.

The 1919 Versailles Conference was a decisive moment in the history of our time, for it provided the victorious powers with a chance to achieve peace on a moral basis. The initial treaty, drafted by President Woodrow Wilson, was a wise and far-sighted document. But fear and opportunism determined the outcome. The Germans were betrayed, and a legacy of bitterness was left. Thirty years of disorder followed. This was not an inevitable outcome. Indeed, it is treated by Johnson as Wilson's personal failure: a better president, not necessarily a more 'altruistic' one, might have made a better peace.

Johnson regards all twentieth-century dictators – Nazi, fascist or communist – as having root connections with socialism. After the First World War, he says, the socialist movement split into two, with a nationalist and an internationalist wing.

Mussolini started, and remained, a socialist of the nationalist kind. Hitler, who also opposed the internationalist movement, took a small socialist workers' party and transformed it. He did not, however, support capitalism. He used it. Left-wingers remained in the party. Goebbels, for instance, stayed on the 'left wing' of the party, remaining a socialist till the end of his days.

Continental European countries, apart from Holland, have a more limited history of private enterprise and private ownership. Capitalism came to Germany with the help of the state. In 1917 Lenin imported Ludendorff's 'war socialism' which had so impressed him. But Johnson believes that a new germ of evil was imported by Lenin into Europe in 1917. Until then, European leaders respected – or at least affected to respect – an absolute morality, and were part of a Judaeo-Christian tradition. Lenin introduced relative morality or what Hitler was later to call the 'higher morality of the party'. Leaders learned from each other. Stalin, impressed by Hitler's putsch against the brownshirts, imitated it, killing two million people, just as Hitler, impressed with Lenin's 1917 revolution, used his own party machine to foment civil disorder as a prelude to revolution. At the end of his days Hitler's reciprocated admiration for Stalin caused him to regret that he had not organised a more throughgoing purge of the German middle classes.

These totalitarian years caused an emigration of scholars and writers, fleeing communist or Nazi tyranny (sometimes both), and these émigrés were profoundly influenced by what they had seen. Hayek was already in England, and took British nationality in 1938. Later, in the 1950s, he went to Chicago, where he helped to develop a 'Chicago School' that included Milton Friedman and George Stigler. Hayek's teacher Ludwig von Mises, whose library had been burned by the Nazis, migrated to New York. The scientist and philosopher Michael Polanyi fled, in turn, from communist oppression in Hungary and Nazi oppression in Germany. One of his central concerns was to demolish the concept of the scientific 'planning' of society. He showed, in a seminal study of the Soviet system, that such planning is a myth. In his work, he explored the nature of what he called our 'tacit knowledge', knowledge that cannot be written down formally or can be expressed only in terms of action.

Karl Popper was another refugee. He foresaw the annexation of Austria by the Nazis and escaped to New Zealand where he taught philosophy throughout the war. He was lucky. Though he had a Protestant upbringing, he would have been regarded by the Nazis as a Jew. An earlier refugee was a remarkable woman called Ayn Rand who had come from the Soviet Union to the USA in 1926. She found success through her novels *The Fountainhead* (1943) and *Atlas Shrugged* (1957), which had a great impact in America, and in the 1970s a growing band of young academics started to develop her ideas. But, in the immediate aftermath of the war, these émigrés were a small scattered band with unpopular ideas, and with no way of linking up.

The high-water mark of the socialist ideal in Western Europe was the British Labour Government which won office at the close of the Second World War. The victory of the Labour Party was more than a simple electoral score. The experience of the inter-war years had left even the most untutored with the impression that markets were not competent to generate wealth or avoid depressions. The state was now seen as a benign and rational head that could co-ordinate the arms and lungs of the nation to achieve fair and agreed objectives. Just as a war economy could be directed to a specific purpose, so could the state in peace. The National Health Service, state secondary schools, the National Coal Board, British Railways and all the other state monopolies created by Herbert Morrison were the tangible form of ideas that had been gaining in popular appeal for a long time. The Beveridge Report, from which most of the arms of the welfare state grew, was a modest essay in Keynesianism. Sir William Beveridge accepted the typically English view that capitalism would survive if it could be modified to provide social security and full employment. He argued that the basic policy of post-war government should be 'freedom from want', secured by a 'plan for social security'. All 'essential liberties' would be preserved.[10]

Without a war the British welfare state would never have been established. The great collective effort of the war had conditioned the population. Public institutions and controls set up in wartime were taken over. Intellectually Britain's post-war revolution was never called to account. It was, as Lord Harris puts it, a 'boy scouts' rally'. 'Its hope was that good will would solve all problems.' Winston Churchill spoke for Tory landowners, evoking shires and cottages and an ethos of semi-feudal concern. Clement Attlee spoke with a voice of intelligent social concern, which evoked his past as a social worker in the East End of London. These two middle-class constituencies had no need to fall out. Indeed they had much in common. By a bit of luck someone had come up with a good idea that made it possible to have a welfare state and keep most of what you had already got. British socialism put the language of Harold Laski round the ideas of Maynard Keynes. And it did not displease the Tories either.

Keynes's *The General Theory of Employment, Interest and Money* (1936) had been written during the slump of the 1930s; this slump was the very image of what the civilised post-war world would now avoid. He had argued that the high levels of unemployment were caused by an excess of 'liquidity' in the economy. People did not have the confidence to invest long term, choosing to keep their cash savings liquid when that money should have been putting people to work. This could be remedied by state action. For the state could manipulate interest rates or invest directly, closing the investment gap, taking the slack out of the system and putting people back to work. Keynes, though, was not as interventionist as his followers. He believed that a large part of government's effect lay in its example, changing the climate of expectation and making private savers readier to sacrifice liquidity.

Wartime had introduced the notion of planning and it had

worked, enabling Britain to win the greatest struggle of all time. Now the Beveridge Report, the 1944 Education Act, the Town and Country Planning Movement represented a peace-time phase of the great project. After a war against fascism came a more comfortable war against poverty. People had dreamed of a time after the war when life would be different and they believed it could be achieved by governments. John Maynard Keynes had invented the new economics which told governments how they could determine the performance of their economies. Classical economics was dead.

In the United States, the New Deal of Roosevelt was continued by President Harry Truman, but the welfare reforms that captivated British politics were mostly deferred until the Great Society years of the Kennedy–Johnson era. Nevertheless, Washington acquainted itself with that new body of skills which enables central authorities to co-ordinate resources. The Tennessee Valley Authority and other civil engineering works were offered as the tangible expression of American socialism. Huge hydroelectric schemes in the Soviet Union were admired by some Americans long after the US government had ceased to talk to Stalin.

Although Truman rapidly cleared the New Dealers out of his Cabinet, in the intellectual sphere the post-war 'liberal consensus' was firmly in place, inspired by the great collective effort of the Second World War. The American literary critic Lionel Trilling was able to assert, without fear of contradiction: 'In the United States at this time, liberalism is not only the dominant but even the sole intellectual tradition. For it is the plain fact that there are no conservative or reactionary ideas in general circulation.'[11]

In 1944, Keynes was at the height of his power and influence, though nearing the end of his life. He was a good and affectionate friend of Hayek, and helped him in a number of ways, such as finding him rooms at Cambridge during the war. In 1943 we find Keynes, on board ship, writing Hayek a letter and commenting on Hayek's latest book.[12] Keynes is bound for Bretton Woods, where he will help to fashion the

International Monetary Fund and the World Bank. Confident of his executive seat on the board of the future, Keynes speaks with the assurance of a man whose ideas have reached dominance. He calls Hayek 'quixotic'. (Why, is he tilting at fantasies?) Yet he assures him at length in the letter that they share the same values. Keynes believes that 'moderate planning' is their best defence – and for thirty years moderate planning was to become the consensus of the age, embodying the underlying ethos of the post-war revolution: management by an intelligent elite.

The first of the key texts in the emergence of new ideas was Frederick Hayek's *The Road to Serfdom,* published in 1944. It was the book that Keynes had been reviewing on board ship. Hayek had written it, his first 'political' book, because he hated the direction British policy was taking. The book argued that although the rhetorical flourishes of fascists and communists might be different, their totalitarian aims were not. Moreover, totalitarianism is the destination to which socialism, even democratic socialism, declines or decays. His clarion was clearly tuned for a bored and indifferent audience. 'We are rapidly abandoning not the views merely of Cobden and Bright, of Adam Smith and Hume, or even of Locke and Milton . . . but the basic individualism inherited by us from Erasmus and Montaigne, from Cicero and Tacitus, Pericles and Thucydides is progressively relinquished.'[13]

Hayek's alarm merely perplexed his readers. Churchill quoted his book, describing the Labour Party as 'Hitler's Heirs', but in those days it sounded risible. The ambitions of democratic socialists were cosy and blameless. Free school milk and medical prescriptions seemed neither oppressive nor servile. The title of the book was meant to suggest that even within the democracies of the West a process was underway in which important personal liberties were being extinguished. He argued that these liberties were not being diminished by a revolutionary conspiracy or coup d'état but by a slow gradual process. There is an immense diversity about human purposes. Those human purposes cannot be ranked on a single scale. Hence the claim that in the long run an attempt to plan an economy centrally must be fatal to individual liberty.

The arguments of *The Road to Serfdom* were rejected and derided by the intelligentsia, although – to Hayek's surprise – the book had a considerable popular success both in Britain and in the USA. George Orwell, his faith in communism broken by his experience in the Spanish Civil War, was one of the few intellectuals to take Hayek seriously. At the time that *Animal Farm* and *1984* were germinating he read *The Road to Serfdom* and reviewed it: 'By bringing the whole of life under the control of the State, Socialism necessarily gives power to an inner ring of bureaucrats, who in almost every case will be men who want power for its own sake and will stick at nothing in order to retain it.'[14] But *The Road to Serfdom*, like *1984*, was not a book that could be said to have predicted the future of the West, even if it is where a movement started. It is a book that looks backwards at the awful history of our century, musing upon the nature of the enemy. The serfdom to come was more subtle and oblique.

The book was also, one suspects, a chance for Hayek to settle his scores with the Fabian socialism of his youth. The Fabians took their name from the Roman general Fabius Cunctator or 'delayer'. Fabius won his campaigns by wearing down the enemy. Fabian socialists put their hopes on the permeation of existing institutions, concentrating on the practical reforms nicknamed 'gas and water socialism.' Their influence on the forming of the British welfare state was great. Hayek enjoyed pointing up the close sympathy between Fabians, like the Webbs, and Tory imperialists in their liking for large and powerful political units.[15] Beatrice Webb coined the phrase 'unassuming experts' to describe the sort of people needed to run the new model state.

Surprised by the success of his book and appalled by the dominance of left-wing ideas in academic life, Hayek believed the best service he could provide for liberalism was to create a movement, connecting up the few isolated liberals who still held positions in academic life. Hayek the activist rallied these other sailors with his megaphone. He found a patron in Switzerland and, with modest resources, established a society of intellectuals opposed to state socialism. He wanted to call it the 'De Tocqueville/Acton Society', but the membership could not agree. Meeting at Mont Pelerin near Geneva in Switzerland in 1947, they settled on the name of this venue for the title of their discreet fraternity.

The Society has met most years since the war. With just 500 members, it is still a small cohort. The media have scarcely been aware of the informal network that links the counter-revolutionaries. Hayek's conferences would anyway have been dismissed as little more than a collection of quaint Edwardian remnants, old fogeys, loyal to classical economics and nineteenth-century liberal values, completely out of the mainstream of intellectual life.

Max Hartwell, the historian of the Mont Pelerin Society, opens an unpublished history with punctilious modesty:

> Between April 1 and 10, 1947, a group of liberals met in the Hotel du Parc on Mont Pelerin, sur Vevey, in Switzerland, to discuss liberalism and its decline, the possibility of a liberal revival, and the desirability of forming an association of people who shared 'certain common convictions' about the nature of a free society.[16]

Hayek was the first president and organiser of the first meeting. Among those present were Karl Popper, Michael Polanyi, Lionel Robbins, who first brought Hayek to England, and Ludwig von Mises. Years later, Milton Friedman, who along with George Stigler was one of the youngest participants, led us through his photograph album, taking special care to point out his 'revered teacher', Frank Knight of the University of Chicago. 'For people who, in their home bases, were isolated,' says Friedman, 'who were in a minority, who were always having to look behind to see if they were going to be stabbed in the back, there was a week in which they might have all sorts of disagreements, where they could be open and above board.' Fund-raising for the first meeting had not come up to expectations and earlier plans to produce a journal were shelved. Dr Albert Hunold raised money from Swiss sources for the costs of accommodation and European travel. The William Volker Charities Trust of Kansas City paid the travel costs of the Americans. There were thirty-nine participants, from ten countries, including seventeen from the USA. Twenty of those present were professional economists.

Hayek was especially concerned to get a German contingent to the meeting. This was difficult because it was still necessary for Germans to obtain permission to travel from the occupying authority. In the end only Walter Eucken of the University of Freiburg got there. Earlier, in a speech in 1944, when he was first canvassing the idea of an association and a journal, Hayek had argued that the 'future of Europe will be largely decided by what will happen in Germany'. He wanted to promote an international discussion about Germany that would be 'more profitable than the "war guilt" bickerings of the last war', and do something towards rescuing Germany, intellectually and morally, regaining it for 'those values on which European civilisation had been built'. The facts of the Nazi regime had to be examined and analysed, and the Germans had to acknowledge their reality. 'I cannot see that the most perfect respect for truth is any way incompatible with the application of very rigorous moral standards in our judgement of historical events,' he said.[17]

At the first meeting these men (and one woman) discussed the nature of liberalism. What were its principles? Why had it declined? How should it be changed? What is the 'competitive order' and how can it be maintained? How are social problems to be solved, especially the problem of poverty? What forces mould political beliefs?

The Society made important links with politicians. Among its members have been Ludwig Erhard, Adenauer's finance minister, a man with a good claim to be the author of Germany's 'economic miracle'. Enoch Powell, Sir Keith Joseph and Sir Geoffrey Howe have provided the link to the British Conservative Party. Arthur Burns, one-time chairman of

America's Federal Reserve Board and later US ambassador to Bonn, was a member too. But its most important effect has been to help rescue from isolation some of the most brilliant minds of our century and give them a common project, the reinvention of liberalism for our time.

Hayek believed that if the flame of liberalism were to be kept as a living ember, capable of being blown into a fire in the future, it had to forego any effort to influence direct political action until the root ideas of liberalism had recovered their strength. In 1944, an Englishman called Antony Fisher, while still a fighter pilot, had read *The Road to Serfdom* in *Reader's Digest*. Being a man who, as he puts it, 'is a bit of a doer', Fisher called Hayek at the London School of Economics and went to his office in the 'same dark corridor as Harold Laski'. Hayek told him not to go into politics. First, said Hayek, a liberal has to make an 'intellectual case amongst intellectuals for what you believe in'.

Some time in the next few years two things happened that helped Fisher to formulate a plan. First, he learned about tax-exempt organisations, having written a paper for a small institute in the USA. Second, he asked Ralph Harris, a lecturer from St Andrews University in Scotland, to come and talk to the Lewes Conservative Party. Walking Harris back to the station, he told him his idea for a small policy institute. Harris told Fisher to call him if he ever got it off the ground.

In 1953 one of Fisher's business projects came good. The Buxted Chicken company was the product of a lucky decision to give up work in the City and concentrate on his Sussex farm. Helped by the first profit of this venture, he started the Institute of Economic Affairs. In 1957 Ralph Harris and Arthur Seldon began working permanently for the Institute.

Harris had found that his views were not, as he puts it, in the 'cockpit of politics'. They certainly did not win him friends in the Common Room at St Andrews. At that time, only a few 'stubborn liberals', like John Jewkes, another Mont Pelerin member, were arguing that although planning in wartime may have looked easy, planning for peace would be much harder. In the hopeful atmosphere of the post-war world, 'freedom' was a marginal issue, associated with eccentrics like Waldron Smithers MP, who campaigned against rationing.

Lord Harris (as he became in 1979), once described as 'the last person in the Western world to part his hair in the middle', confesses to being an old-fashioned Liberal. He laments the total disappearance of the old Liberal Party from British politics at the turn of the century when it tried to 'dish' the expanding Labour Party and lost its soul in the process. Determined to pre-empt the rise of Labour, the Liberals introduced health insurance, welfare proposals and the illiberal Trades Disputes Act of 1906, which gave unions immunity from civil damages. This exemption was unique in the West. Even the Webbs regarded it as 'an extraordinary and unprecedented immunity'. After that the Whig tradition went missing for sixty years.

When the Institute of Economic Affairs was eventually formed it had the advantage of well-wishers like Lord Robbins, those who had actually been involved in wartime planning. Robbins knew at first hand that political decisions are not made in calm and serenely minuted meetings. He knew the difficulties of getting decisions out of ministers who were always rushing off somewhere else. The IEA also set an important trend, becoming the first of many policy institutes around the world, a lot of them assisted at their birth by Antony Fisher, their links with Mont Pelerin preserved by placing society members on the advisory boards. The appeal of the IEA lies in its eschewal of propaganda and in its determination not to adhere to any particular party. That gave it the opportunity to speak to Conservatives when the need arose.

In 1964, thirteen years of Tory rule came to an end, and the Institute received a visit from Keith Joseph, who revealed that his first spell in government had taught him that it was 'difficult to achieve good results'. Harris and Seldon set out a display of pamphlets, which Joseph walked round like a 'buyer at a fair'. He might have seen a pamphlet called *Saving in a Free Society* written by Enoch Powell, who, as a young Treasury Minister, had resigned with the rest of the Treasury team on the issue of public spending in 1958. Powell moved to the periphery of Conservative politics after his anti-immigration speeches in the 1960s.

In 1970 the government of Edward Heath took office with a commitment to new free-market policies, but the initiative soon collapsed. When unemployment reached a million, Heath engineered a spending spree; his anti-union legislation was ill-conceived; and the 1974 miners' strike finally brought his government down. The IEA was initially enthusiastic about Heath – after all, his 1963 law against resale price maintenance, or protecting what Americans would call 'shoppers' choice', had been inspired by the first IEA pamphlet, so beginning a growing, often critical, IEA involvement with Conservative policy. But disenchantment set in and the Institute predicted the 1976 inflation that followed his 1973 boom, an inflation which sent the (by then) Labour government off to the International Monetary Fund. As a policy unit the IEA had been blooded in the Heath era. That government's failure enabled the Institute to identify its two major interests: union power and monetary policy. In 1975 Keith Joseph came back for a 'further course of education'.

'It was a direct reaction to the frustrations and disappointments of office,' remembers Harris, 'of seeing our competitive position deteriorate, of seeing the welfare services under constant pressure. You could never spend enough on health and education to satisfy the increasing demands of the populace for better or more services. The unemployment figure rose, constantly, with a ratchet effect, never falling back to the old level, and then in the trough the figure went higher. For Keith Joseph it was a pragmatic matter. The existing policies – the consensus, as it came to be characterised – hadn't worked. Alternative policies were necessary.' Keith Joseph was the architect of the liberal revival that won control of the Conservative Party. Starting with a lecture at Preston in 1974, he began to make controversial statements on employment policy and on social policy which led away from the old centre ground. They drew much personal criticism, and after a period of self-appraisal, Joseph decided not to stand for party leader. Mrs Thatcher assumed his mantle when he stood down.

In recent years the Institute has turned its attention to 'public choice' theory, the study of how public decisions are made and influenced by the political structure. It is an important arm of New Enlightenment thinking. Lord Harris's most 'depressing' afternoons, he told us, are on Wednesdays, when he attends the House of Lords, sitting as a cross-bencher. 'It is despairing', he says, 'to see how policy is decided in a democratic assembly.' He observes the power of pressure groups and special interests, noting that a wraith-like entity like the Church of England can halt the liberalisation of shop-opening hours, even though that reform is supported by 67 per cent of the population.

Antony Fisher went on to help form other institutes. He helped fund the Frazer Institute in Canada, worked hard to set up the Manhattan Institute in New York. Then came the Pacific Foundation in San Francisco, the Centre for Independent Studies in Australia, and many more. Today there are over thirty institutes in seventeen countries, including Argentina, France and Spain. They seek to make an impact on policy and have won many legislative initiatives since that time in 1963 when the Conservatives stopped manufacturers from fixing retail prices.

The relationship between ideas and events is obscure. It may be true, as Keynes says, that most 'practical men' are the slaves of some 'defunct economist', but what matters most is the moment when practical men change their minds. Politicians have a pressing need to get things right. The decline of a fashionable theory does not lose a professorship, but a mistake can wreck a government, lose an election or ruin a country. If you look carefully at the history of the post-war world you soon realise that the 'liberal consensus' which Lionel Trilling described as the 'sole international tradition' was more an accord among intellectuals than a political reality.

By 1945 the American political establishment was totally disillusioned with Stalin. There had been New Dealers who admired the Soviet Union's achievements and wanted an accord. But Stalin's greed and opportunism – the breaking of his word on free elections in Poland, the post-war purges in the Balkan States – changed all that. Before he died, Roosevelt recognised the scale of his earlier misjudgement; 'We can't do business with Stalin,' he had said. By March 1946, Churchill had made the Iron Curtain speech, and the last New Dealer, Henry Wallace, was expelled from Truman's Cabinet. Wallace had advocated unilateral disarmament and a massive aid programme for Russia. While the British were engrossed in their social welfare experiment, and with the dismantling of their empire, the Americans turned away from collectivism.

One admirer of the British experiment was J. K. Galbraith. He was an acolyte of Keynes and a profound believer in 'intelligent planning'. His sympathies were with the New Dealers, purged from post-war administrations in the USA and not to reappear until the Kennedy years. In his best-selling book *The Affluent Society* (1958) he compared the 'private affluence' and 'public squalor' of American life. He had been a wartime planner, working on price control, and he thought such techniques should be carried over into post-war America. He encouraged governments to develop incomes policies. In a later work he developed the idea of the 'techno-structure', a codeword for a system in which all important innovation and new product development comes from the research departments of big public companies whose power enables them to control markets and supply them with new products when they choose. Old-fashioned entrepreneurs were irrelevant in this new corporate business world.

The most successful post-war economies outside the United States had to reconstruct themselves from rubble in 1945, working under new liberal constitutions prepared by British and American advisers. They too started their post-war lives outside the fashionable social democratic consensus and away from the spell of the British welfare state. In the 1949 German general election, the British Labour government supported the Social Democrats under Schumacher, who wanted to unite Germany on Bismarckian lines and build an all-powerful paternalist state. Dr Konrad Adenauer, Germany's great post-war leader, had a very different vision. For him, the antithesis of national socialism (his daughter said he used to pray every night for Hitler's defeat) was 'individualism'. He did not think the reunification of Germany was practical. Instead he worked for a smaller Germany, with 'windows wide open to the West'. Adenauer brought on to his Cabinet team Ludwig Erhard, whose free-market philosophy, based on low tariffs, free trade and cheap imports, exactly suited his own ideas. The New Germany was to be founded not on the redistribution of wealth (there wasn't any), but on sharing in growth.

But nothing helped to undermine support for the corporate state more than the decline of Britain. In the 1950s, Britain's stock stood high and had the approval of progressives world-wide. But by the early 1960s the British economy was failing badly against its neighbours. This was crushingly brought home to the British in 1967, when De Gaulle vetoed British entry to the Common Market, pointing to chronic weaknesses in the British economy (British gross national product per head was overtaken by those of France and Germany in the 1960s). From this point the reconstruction of the British economy became the major preoccupation of British political life, leading to the technocratic reforms introduced by Harold Wilson, the union reforms attempted by Wilson and Heath and the adoption of explicit free-market economics by Margaret Thatcher.

The welfare state came late to the United States. It was fully embodied, however, in Lyndon Johnson's Great Society, that dynamic phase of legislative activity in the mid-1960s. The Great Society welfare programme rested on state intervention of an order unprecedented in American life. As Theodore White says, civil rights legislation aimed to do no less than 'change the customs and manners of the American people'.[18] In the summer of 1968 blacks and students – both the subjects of beneficent intervention by the state – took action in their own right in a revolution of rising expectations. Middle America did not like what it saw. Soon other disturbing reports began to come in from the undergrowth of the new welfare society. America turned its face away again.

In the 1970s the Western world had to face a devastating new problem: inflation. It took a crisis to bring new ideas into government, and that was the price-inflation that followed the 1973 Arab–Israeli war. It gave a cue to that group of economists who became known as the monetarists. Foremost among them was Milton Friedman, who, almost unrecognisable among the felt hats and raincoats, appears in the inaugural photographs of the first meeting of the Mont Pelerin Society back in 1947.

By 1979 US citizens were listing 'inflation' as the major issue in the coming presidential race. In the last year of Jimmy Carter's presidency, inflation had risen to double digits. The cost of the Great Society programmes (increased by the indexing of social security payments to the cost of living in 1972) was prompting massive public sector deficits, which were clearly inflationary. In 1973, the Arab–Israeli war had exposed the US's vulnerability to imported oil. Prices rose inexorably through the decade. Even food went up in real terms, pushed by the growing world demand for the USA's food surpluses. In the USA labour unions were not seen as a cause of inflationary pressure. On the contrary, in 1980 the real wages of working families actually dropped by 5 per cent, indicating a labour market flexibility that was the envy of the Europeans, but giving a sharp jolt to ordinary Americans' living standards. They identified inflation as the cause. In the work of Friedman and his colleagues, politicians found a new approach to the problem. Friedman argued that inflation was caused by an excess supply of money, not just cash, but the whole gamut of short- and medium-term credits which an economist describes as 'money'. This excess supply was caused, for instance, by governments who 'printed' money by injecting demand when unemployment was rising.

In Britain inflation was more likely to be seen as the sign of a society that could not keep its promises or handle the tensions within that society, a sign of the failure of a state that offers a 'fair' distribution of rewards. It proved impossible to agree on what was 'fair', and powerful competing groups chased prices up. In the second half of the 1970s the collapse of wage control undermined Labour's Social Contract with the unions and brought the Conservatives back into office. Inflationary pressures had been working away in Britain's inefficient economy. Repeated attempts to recharge the economy by easy money policies led to inflationary pressures, trade deficits, and retreats bringing back policies of price or pay restraint. This cycle came to be known as 'Stop–Go'. It resulted in a kind of economic paroxysm.

The monetarists developed a detailed critique of contemporary policy, in particular of the notion that you could buy yourself out of recession. As the impetus behind Keynesian state planning was an attack on unemployment caused by under-investment, so Milton Friedman developed the counter-notion of a 'natural rate of unemployment'. That is the rate to which an economy naturally reverts unless it receives greater and greater fiscal stimuli and, in consequence, rapid and ever increasing inflation. These ideas became important with the dramatic collapse of the so-called 'Phillips curve' which proposed a trade-off between unemployment and inflation and which had supposedly given planners a reliable tool for economic management. Suddenly socialism lost its intellectual assurance. By 1972, inflation and unemployment were both increasing. Britain had a textbook impossibility – stagflation.

The first senior Conservative convert to monetarist policy was Sir Keith Joseph, influenced by Professors Alan Walters and Peter Bauer of the London School of Economics, and by a renewed acquaintance with the work of the Institute of Economic Affairs under Ralph Harris. Joseph's Preston speech of

1974 first developed the view that inflation would have to be countered by allowing a rise in the rate of unemployment. He said that unemployment figures overstated the real number of those available for work in the labour market. Such views were heresy. Edward Heath regarded the speech most unfavourably and was not at all keen about the establishment of the Centre for Policy Studies by Margaret Thatcher, Keith Joseph and Geoffrey Howe. Alfred Sherman, a right-wing journalist, became full-time director.

In a separate strand of development, two journalists, Peter Jay of *The Times* and Samuel Brittan of the *Financial Times*, began importing monetarist ideas from the US. Contrary to popular belief, the first ministerial convert to monetarism in Britain was not Margaret Thatcher, but the Labour Chancellor, Denis Healey. And at the Labour Conference in 1976, Prime Minister Callaghan appeared to disavow any lingering belief in the efficiency of demand management. 'You cannot spend your way out of a recession,' he said, in a speech supposedly drafted by his then son-in-law, Peter Jay.

By the end of the 1970s both Ronald Reagan and Margaret Thatcher were seeking office with new liberal economic policies. They had been adopted to deal with economies that were getting out of hand. That was the tear in the curtain which allowed liberalism back on the stage. Yet, although inflation and monetarism were such lively issues in the 1970s, they play little further part in our story.

Ronald Reagan was the first American President to have an economics degree. We do not have to ask where his classical ideas came from. Ronald Reagan had finished his studies at Eureka College, Illinois, before his teachers had heard of John Maynard Keynes. Later in life he made his mark inside the Republican Party as a free-enterprise speech-maker for General Electric. By the time he reached the 1980 campaign, his intellectual team consisted of Martin Anderson, Richard Allen and William Buckley. Martin Anderson, who described himself as a 'libertarian', had come to rest in California's Hoover Institution. It was in California that he met Ronald Reagan and from there he guided him to the leadership of the growing minority who were in revolt against the dominant 'liberal' ideas that reigned on campus. It was Martin Anderson who drafted Reagan's first policy memo in 1979, basing it on the premise that inflation was the main domestic problem facing the US. The Reagan programme was not as concerned about controlling the money supply as the British had been. It offered a 'supply-side' plan, concentrating on controlling federal spending and liberating economic growth. It promised a reduction in federal taxes and the elimination of 'counterproductive regulation'. 'There were five key elements,' says Martin Anderson, speaking of the policy memo he helped to draft.

> One, we had to reduce the growth of federal spending. Two, we needed to reduce tax rates. [He decided specifically on 10 per cent for three years.] Three, we had to change and reform government regulation. (In fact, one of the most important things that happened in the United States during the last five years has been the new regulations that were not proposed.) Four, we needed a more stable monetary policy. And five, probably the most important part of the Reagan economic programme, was stability. He said, whatever programme we begin, whatever economic strategy we pursue, let us not change it, let us keep it constant, so that people have a chance to get used to it, and have confidence it will remain the same.

Martin Anderson's intellectual evolution follows a pattern that will be repeated often. As a young man he started to study the effects of government housing programmes, but found the opposite of what he had expected. 'The more I got into it,' he says,

> the more I discovered that what people thought about the programme just wasn't true. The result of a programme whose initial purpose was to help Americans achieve better homes and better living environments was destroying four times as many homes as it was building. What was most

> unconscionable was that it was destroying the homes of low-income, mostly black people. The buildings that it did create were homes for upper- and high-income people. This was a classic example of a government programme with good intentions that was achieving just the opposite of what it wanted, at enormous cost to the taxpayer.

Anderson described his discoveries in a book called *The Federal Bulldozer* (1964). It is a case study in the law of unintended consequences. There will be more in this book about the failure of good intentions.

In Britain, many intelligent people had thought a distinction could be made between political and economic freedom. That assumption was at the heart of democratic socialism with its promise of civil liberty and economic restraint. But what has happened in post-war Britain is more subtle than what Frederick Hayek or George Orwell warned about. In the real 1984, Britain was a moderately stable country with extensive civil liberties. The threat to our freedom came not from political oppression, but from economic failure. This failure has meant diminishing possibilities, a poverty you cannot get away from, a cramping sense of promise unfulfilled, coalitions of the strong against the weak, dependence for millions. Men like Paul Johnson, who was once editor of the left-wing *New Statesman*, have come to consider democratic socialism a contradiction in terms. 'If you start to tamper with economic freedom, you find things don't work very well,' Johnson now says. 'You go further and further, trying to get the results you want, until you run into resistance from people. To beat that resistance you have to limit freedom.'

The effects of failure are diffuse. They touch our freedoms not like a policeman's hand on the shoulder, but like a progressive illness that one tries to pretend is not there. The ideal of the British welfare state vanished in the Winter of Discontent when public sector workers struck against the weak and unrepresented. Social democratic Britain became a country of multiple small conspiracies against the future. A place of stasis and opportunities missed. The socialist idea has died many times in many places. When Irving Kristol graduated from City College, New York, in 1940, he was a member of the Young People's Socialist League.

> Socialism could remain a very attractive idea so long as there were not many socialist governments. But once you have socialist government in the world and you're looking at socialist reality as distinct from socialist ideality, you realise it doesn't work very well. Its assumptions about human nature and the incentives necessary to move people, particularly in the economic field, are false and utopian. The reality of socialism has been utterly disillusioning. There isn't a single socialist country in this world to which one can point and say, that's a good model for us, that's the kind of country we want to be like.

For the first eighty years of this century, the left has been in the ascendant. Those who argued for rationalism and planning in human affairs put their faith in the power of the state. Socialism enjoyed the support of most intellectuals. Now, under the patronage of Margaret Thatcher and Ronald Reagan, the liberal revival is enjoying some success. These two leaders have been carefully watched by New Enlightenment thinkers. There has been disappointment that neither has had any great success at reducing the size of government spending, but recognition that, as Milton Friedman says: 'It is easier to bring that understanding to the world of ideas than it is to translate it into the world of practice.' Friedman thinks their years in government have shown how difficult the liberal project is. 'The central planning idea collapsed, but it didn't mean that government ceased growing. The problem shifted, from a central planning problem to a redistribution problem that came with the welfare state. The one thing government can do is to take money from some and give to others. The threat to freedom is greater today, but the source of that threat is a different one. It is that governments, in their reaction to particular groups that want them to use their powers to take from some and to give to others, will grow without bounds.'

But the new ideas are spreading – to the 'neo-liberal' wing of the Democratic Party in America, or into the 'social market' ideas of David Owen in the Social Democratic Party in Britain. Those who followed Hayek's advice are filling academic chairs and editorial roles. Liberal think-tanks, ranging from the august to the tiny, have captured the academic debate. In Washington the Heritage Foundation is making the running where the Brookings Institute used to; in London the IEA has supplanted the National Institute for Economic and Social Research as an influence on government. These changes are having an increasing effect on public opinion. The challenge to the welfare apparatus and the programmes for deregulation and privatisation were born of pamphlets published a decade ago. New Enlightenment writers now inspire governments. The Frazer Institute in Vancouver advises the government of British Columbia on the abolition of rent control. The Adam Smith Institute of London campaigns for the privatisation of the BBC and the deregulation of British broadcasting. The National Center for Policy Analysis in Dallas produces a paper arguing that the state pension scheme exploits blacks in favour of whites, since it makes no adjustment for their shorter life expectancies.

But something more has been happening these last thirty years than an efflorescence of pamphleteering. The great figures of the New Enlightenment have been writing their major works, laying the foundations of twentieth-century liberalism. And a group of younger men and women, successors to Hayek and Popper, have been doing deep and detailed thinking about the nature of our present and our future. They help us to explain why welfare states make people poor.

2

Serfdom Today

Above this race of men stands an immense and tutelary power, which takes upon itself alone to secure their gratifications, and watch over their fate. That power is absolute, minute, regular, provident, and mild. It would be like the authority of a parent, if, like that authority, its object was to prepare men for manhood; but it seeks on the contrary to keep them in perpetual childhood; it is well content that the people should rejoice, provided they think of nothing but rejoicing. For their happiness a government willingly labours, but it chooses to be the sole agent and the only arbiter of their happiness: it provides for their security, foresees and supplies their necessities, facilitates their pleasures, manages their principal concerns, directs their industry, regulates the descent of property, and subdivides their inheritances – what remains, but to spare them all the care of thinking and all the trouble of living?

Alexis de Tocqueville[1]

The basic offer of a welfare state is exactly what William Beveridge promised: freedom from want, and social security. In Britain, the predominant elements of the welfare state, such as health, education and the relief of poverty, are planned nationally and delivered free. The aim of a 'free' service, paid for out of general taxation, is to impose equality on inequality. The same spirit and general approach inspired the other reforms of Britain's post-war Labour Government which included the nationalisation of basic industries and a programme of full employment. In this chapter we will argue that, in spite of the good intentions of those who champion it, this philosophy does not work.

A policy inspired by this philosophy will tend to set up institutions that help the middle class more than the working class, and give a high standard of service to no one very much. It will set up institutions which will serve the interests of the men and women who work in them better than they serve their customers or clients. Customer choice and customer

The writing of this chapter has been greatly helped by David Green, Sir Reginald Murley, John C. Goodman, James Buchanan, Charles Murray and Irving Kristol.[2]

awareness will be weak. The institutions' own choices about the future are likely to be wrong. It will be poorly informed about people's needs and over-influenced by political pressure. Consider Britain's National Health Service, the prize of the welfare state, once acclaimed 'the envy of the world'.

This is the true story of William Benton.[3] It is a story about the creation of poverty. We do not believe it is particularly unusual. William Benton is now sixty-five. He spent his working life as a shipbuilding worker on Teesside in northern England. When we saw him in March 1986 he had lost the last two years of his working life waiting for an operation which had been inflicted on him by an earlier medical mistake. His stomach was flopping out over his belt and there was a four-inch wide maroon scar from his sternum to his groin. He was in considerable pain, could not even bend over to tie up his shoelaces, and was not eating much. He was not an 'emergency'.

Back in February 1984 he had contracted jaundice and had been to hospital. There he underwent his first operation, having his gall-bladder and some gallstones removed. While recovering in hospital he found that some soup was coming through the stitches in his stomach. He was put back on a drip and kept in hospital for another five days before being discharged. Then he was told a district nurse would come and remove his stitches soon after his return home. He and his wife waited for three weeks, during which time his stomach kept splitting open even though he stayed in bed. Finally they rang their general practitioner. He had not even been told that Mr Benton had been discharged. For the next five months Mr Benton then lived with an open wound which was diagnosed by his general practitioner as an incisional hernia, caused by the gall-bladder operation. Because it was not an 'emergency', his surgeon at the hospital told him he would have to wait. There were thousands of other patients ahead of him and only a few beds. Mr Benton was finally operated on, after a two-year wait, in June 1986. Why was this patient of the NHS so badly served?

Mr Benton's local hospital is in the South Tees Area. In

North Tees, a few minutes' drive away, is a large hospital that is relatively new and relatively under-used. Many think that the decision to build this hospital in 1958 was a 'political' one. They stress the roles of George Chetwynd, who was the Labour MP for Stockton, and of Harold Macmillan (later Lord Stockton), who had once represented the constituency where the hospital was sited. Although it serves only a moderate-size catchment area, it is the largest general hospital in the North of England. The decision to build was taken in 1958. The main 600-bed phase was not complete until 1974. The 1004-bed hospital is now finished.

As it was being built it became clear that there were too many wards for the number of staff. The administration applied pressure for more staff. As the region could not supply them, it was suggested they take on more patients from South Tees along with some South Tees staff. A joint meeting was set up between the medical committees of doctors on both sides. According to a surgeon who has now retired, the meeting broke up when North Tees doctors were accused of trying to take South Tees's private patients. That was the last joint meeting ever held between the two sides. Rivalry and professional antagonism stopped rational discussion about the public interest. Today South Tees doctors do not refer patients to North Tees hospital. An extraordinary situation follows from this. In 1985 North Tees hospital had one of the shortest waiting lists for general surgery in the country – fifty-one. South Tees had one of the largest – 1760. The two hospitals are ten minutes' apart by ambulance.

We were still more surprised when we looked at the number of general surgical beds in South Tees. Was it very short of them? No: in 1984 it had 176 beds. That put it, in terms of provision, in the best 40 per cent of health authorities relative to its size. In terms of consultants, South Tees was better off than 90 per cent of the other authorities in the country. So why was Mr Benton kept waiting? We never got a clear answer. Once more we had to rely on a former surgeon for an explanation. He is a man who had been with the health service from its early days. He told us he had 'little time' for his former colleagues. They had 'forgotten that doctors are made for patients'. The problem with the South Tees surgeons was their 'arrogance'. They reminded him, he said, of the 'Pharisees whose first prayer in the morning was "Thank God I am not as other men".'[4] He suggested that the consultants were not working hard enough. When we asked the hospital administration for an explanation for the delay, we were told that there is an emphasis on 'quality' rather than 'quantity' – meaning, presumably, that a gall-bladder operation falls into the latter category. The administrator of a district has little influence on consultants, who are appointed by the region and enjoy lifetime tenure. We were also told that the delays were caused by a shortage of beds. Mr Benton's own GP has no idea how the hospital 'decides who they are going to see'. Another reason for long waiting lists at South Tees was the industrial disputes of 1979 and 1981. By 1981 the list had risen to 2950.

We asked Mr Benton what he thought the problem was. He thought it must be the 'government' and the 'cuts'. Like most patients of the NHS, Mr Benton has a placid, respectful attitude to doctors. He reminded us that his surgeon had saved his life. Mr Benton is the reason the National Health Service exists.

The truth is that the National Health Service is in terrible shape. The discrepancy in mortality rates between the rich and poor has widened since the NHS started. Costs rise and services decline. Waiting lists for operations grow. Its buildings are poor and badly situated. Patients are shuffled from one queue to another carrying the details of their tests or fluid samples. Doctors' waiting-rooms fill up with people looking at the clock. Advice about specialist care is hard to get. In this failing service doctors have to exercise a cruel discretion. A sixty-five-year-old diabetic must be assessed for his life-value. He may have to be sent home to die for lack of renal dialysis. Britain has fewer renal dialysis centres than any other West European country for which we could find figures. Belgium, Switzerland, Austria, Spain have four times more centres per head of population than Britain. What is more, in Britain doctors' competence goes unchecked. In one survey, only 8 per cent of junior doctors were found able to give a simple heart massage. Another showed that very few doctors could recognise the symptoms of a common ear infection.

The squalor and meanness of the system have grown as rapidly as its consumption of resources. The demarcation of roles is strict. Nurses insist that even household tasks must be done by 'professionals', that is to say by no one but nurses. The aim may be status as much as pay. Catering and cleaning in the NHS are so poor that it exempts itself from the normal laws covering health, safety and hygiene, asserting 'Crown immunity'. A recent survey of 1000 hospital kitchens by the Department of the Environment showed that 600 were breaking food regulations. Ninety-seven were in such a state as to merit prosecution. In 1985 19 people died and 460 were made ill from an outbreak of food poisoning at the Stanely Royd Hospital in Wakefield. It took nine days and thirteen deaths before the health authorities asked the public health authority to look into it. Planning proposals to modernise the kitchens, drawn up in 1978, had still not been implemented seven years later.

The people for whom the NHS (the biggest single employer in Europe) exists are powerless. They are pauperised, treated as supplicants, not as customers. GPs in the NHS earn 'capitation' fees, depending for their pay on the numbers of patients registered with them. Patients cannot see their notes. Hospital staff prefer glamorous operations to the prosaic needs of powerless patients. Pedro Schwartz, a Spanish economist observing the British NHS, invented this wry dictum: 'The private sector is that part of the economy controlled by the government; the public sector is that part controlled by nobody.'[5] Sure enough, when the recent Griffiths Report (1982) asked NHS hospital staff to point to a single individual or committee which was in charge, they could not do so.[6]

As the lack of dialysis units shows, Britain's standards of

health care, by international standards, are very poor. Britain is unique in the developed world as a country where the incidence of heart disease has continued to increase. It now has the highest death rate in the world from this disease. Deaths from cervical cancers are almost as high as they were fifteen years ago, although other European countries have halved the rate. Further, expectation of life at forty-five is one of the worst for any developed country. Britain's ten-year mortality surveys continue to show huge differences in the expected lifespan of different groups and classes. Yet doctors are highly regarded members of the community.[7] Very few people complain about the standards of health care they get. The NHS has a monopoly. Its patients do not know any different.

Many analyses have been made of the failure of the National Health Service. They usually blame someone. Some allege that failure is due to a miserly government, since the British now spend less per capita on health than any other country in Europe. Others blame managerial failures and devise intricate new management systems according to the latest graduate business school craze. The power of the doctors is often mentioned. The analysis we offer for the failure of the National Health Service is a different one. It does not 'blame' anyone in particular. We rely heavily on the work of Dr David Green, once a Labour councillor of Newcastle-upon-Tyne, and now a specialist in health economics.[8]

In 1981 David Green took up a post at the Australian National University. While there he began researching into Australian welfare and came across the Australian friendly societies. He found that these self-supporting mutual-aid societies provided high-quality low-cost medical care. Some even had their own hospitals. He learned that most of these organisations were branches of similar societies that had flourished in the UK before the formation of the NHS. On returning to Britain, he studied the friendly societies and found that many of them had been formed, owned and run by working-class people. The South Wales miners, for instance, had set up numerous medical aid societies, which they themselves controlled through elected committees.

Something else influenced him while in Australia. That was the way his wife was treated by private doctors. Back in Gateshead she had been made to wait in an antenatal clinic along with twenty other women; they never saw the doctor in whose nominal charge they had been placed, and spent hours standing round semi-naked, waiting to undergo one test or another. In Australia her experience was dramatically different. After conferring with other mothers, she made her choice of obstetrician. He offered a personal service, discussing methods of delivery, whether pain-killers would be used, foetal heart monitoring applied and so on. Both the receptionist and her obstetrician remembered her name. As a mark of respect for her dignity, a sheet was placed over her legs during internal examinations.

David Green gathered information about the early history of public medical services in Britain. Back in 1911, many doctors in Britain were employed by mutual-aid associations. Branches elected doctors after negotiations on prices and the quality of service. In 1911 the British government ordered that all men in work be enrolled in a national insurance scheme. Women and children were excluded. For them, as for everyone not catered for by the mutual-aid societies before 1911, there was a range of charity and municipal hospitals. The earlier system was a long way from perfect. But it was better than we have been led to believe. And it was improving. The original pressure for the 1911 scheme came from those who wanted to make sure that the poor received better care than was currently provided under the Poor Laws. But the bill was hijacked by an alliance of the British Medical Association and the insurance companies and it subsequently required the male working population, three-quarters of whom had already joined friendly societies, to register on a 'panel' with a general practitioner.

The doctors had demanded a high price for their inclusion in the new national panel system – in particular they insisted on more money and a limit to organised consumer choice. The panel was the beginning of the doctor's list as a basis for his remuneration. Though mutual-aid societies struggled to continue and showed considerable vitality, they were put under great disabilities by the state system. Right up to the foundation of the NHS in 1948 efforts were being made to set up new ones, but in that year the mutual-aid societies and friendly societies were phased out altogether.

The doctors now exacted a higher price for their co-operation. The doctors' union, the BMA, increased its powers. The regulation of the profession fell to the General Medical Council, which was 'captured' by doctors, by far the largest group. The GMC, which has increased its powers steadily since it was established in 1858, regulates the training of doctors and sets entry requirements. It comprises ninety-five members, eighty-four of whom are 'elected' by the medical profession. The elections are dominated by nominees of the BMA. The BMA is a trade union, a guild with a monopoly supply of labour, though like other 'professional' associations, such as the Law Society, it finds that analogy a slur. It has won good terms for its members, such as the unlimited tenure of hospital consultants. It defends the right of consultants to take private patients. Yet it has often been pointed out that, if a doctor takes private patients, there is an incentive to keep a long waiting list that encourages patients to pay for their operations.

The GMC thus became the controlling body of the profession. It keeps a register of 'competent' persons; once they have passed their medical exams and graduated from medical school, they are not subsequently tested. It has resisted the pressure for reviews, in spite of surveys like the one reported above which show that some doctors do not know routine procedures. When the NHS was founded, only doctors on the medical register were permitted to serve in it. The consumer was denied the choice of 'alternative' medicines within the NHS.

The GMC's code of ethics is, in many respects, a code of

restrictive practices. It bans advertising or canvassing for 'ethical' reasons, though this would be one way for customers to find out that a certain doctor has a particular approach to an illness or the resources to perform this or that test. The GMC is exempt from the requirements of the Restrictive Trades Practices Act. It has control of 'professional misconduct', which is left as a matter for the GMC to define. Doctors often refuse to testify against each other. The system has not made doctors rich, but it rewards them in other ways, such as providing unearned leisure and high status, and it has protected them from the costs of negligence.

Sir Reginald Murley has had a lifetime's involvement with the NHS and has watched its decline from the first flush of enthusiasm to the desperate straits of the present. In 1977 he was elected President of the Royal College of Surgeons and in 1979 he was knighted. He is one of the few doctors willing to speak out on the failure of the NHS. Back in 1948, he was told by a doctor whom he respected that the NHS would be carried for the first twenty-five years by the traditions that were already established. Then the 'cracks' would begin to show. Sir Reginald now sees a service beset by 'union problems' and restrictive practices. 'When you have a single paymaster you forget you are performing a service for an individual. . . . With the government as your paymaster, things change,' he says. Many anaesthetists, for instance, are contracted to do ten sessions a week. But over the years their representatives have negotiated an arrangement that one session is counted away for getting to work, another for pre-operative assessment, another for post-operative assessment, another for writing up records, and another for emergency cover, when they do not always have to come in. That leaves five sessions for patients. So . . . the cut-off time for 'cold surgery' moves from 7 p.m. to 6 p.m. to 5 p.m. while waiting lists grow. An occasional practice becomes a permanent practice and step by step the system declines. People have come to accept, says Sir Reginald, 'very poor standard of service' because a state monopoly of medicine leaves them nothing to compare it with. 'State medicine is a form of state-subsidised mediocrity.'

Sir Reginald believes that the relationship between patient and doctor is a one-to-one relationship in which the state need have no part. While he sees a case for state involvement in public health, drainage, and so on, he sees no case for government involvement in day-to-day medicine. If the state wishes to set minimum standards, or to provide supplementary services, there are 'better ways to do it than by nationalising' medicine. People must, in his view, have more choice. They should not be the 'prisoners of any doctor's list'. He believes that an adequate system of insurance could easily be developed, and that if hospitals were run as private enterprises they would operate more efficiently. Insurance systems have the enormous advantage that they create an incentive for preventive medicine; for example, insurance schemes in America have been successful in reducing the incidence of heart disease. The huge hospitals in the British system seem designed for doctors and staff, not for patients. Grotesque, unanticipated effects occur. In the early days of the NHS Sir Reginald battled to get air-conditioning into operating theatres. Today, hospitals are wholly air-conditioned, something which is quite unnecessary in Britain. Their vents become carriers of legionnaires' disease. Like David Green, Sir Reginald is in favour of a voucher system. That would leave a person free to cash a health voucher in any way he or she chose.

It is customary to point to America as an illustration of how bad a 'private system' is, indifferent to the uninsured, beset by litigation, charging enormous fees. That is fundamentally wrong on two counts. First, Americans have, on the whole, better health care than the British. Second, it is not a fully 'private' system. The evolution of the American health system has in some ways been similar to the British. In both countries, it has been accepted that medicine requires heavy government regulation. Once more, the doctors through their professional association or union, the American Medical Association, gained restrictions on competition and choice. In the United States doctors won control at state, not federal, level. Their power lies in their control of the medical examiners. For the analysis that follows, we are grateful to Dr John Goodman, who is President of the National Center for Policy Analysis in Dallas.[9]

In the nineteenth century almost anyone could become a doctor, set up a hospital or a medical school. The AMA soon made it much more difficult to get into the profession, eliminating half the medical schools and most of the for-profit hospitals. The doctors took over and effectively organised the profession, controlling its size with the result that, over time, the ratio of doctors to the rest of the community fell.

As in Britain the support of the state for the monopoly was vital. The association was able to justify its monopoly control of the supply of doctors by promising to protect the population from 'incompetent', unlicensed doctors, though doing little to control the 'competence' of its members, except by specifying particular medical schools and lengthening the courses. Doctors who had practised before this regime were 'grandfathered' into the profession. For everyone else barriers to entry were raised.

In hospitals doctors remained in charge and operated an inefficient cost-plus pricing structure. They would only work with selected medical insurance companies. Doctors refused to admit new companies, willing to offer better rates, if the companies wished to influence hospital practice, or scrutinise prices.

This remained the general pattern until recently, but in the United States doctor power was a great deal more vulnerable than in the UK. Price control was first to go; doctors can no longer charge what they please. Dissatisfied with the system, companies offering health insurance to their employees became more heavily involved. A company finance director might call a hospital to discuss costs and treatment, and negotiate with the doctor. Recently, Health Maintenance Organisations have begun to flourish. HMOs negotiate a fixed-price contract with a customer to meet all medical costs in a year. In ordinary practice a doctor makes money from a patient's illness. In an HMO the incentive for the doctor is to reduce illness, and to minimise a patient's call on his time. At the end of a year the customer can switch if dissatisfied. Something similar to HMOs had existed at the turn of the century before the AMA got rid of them by denying them malpractice insurance. In the last few years they have grown rapidly. Other new developments in the USA include 'immedi-centers' which provide out-patient and emergency services in competition with hospitals and an increase with for-profit hospitals. New kinds of health services in the USA have been opened up by dissident doctors, pursuing their rights to operate independently all the way to the Supreme Court. The annual increase in the cost of medical care has fallen below the rate of inflation.

David Green, Sir Reginald Murley and John Goodman all agree that the medical services would be greatly improved if monopolies were broken, customer choice re-established, and competition injected back into the system.

What general truths can we identify about the failure of 'free' national health systems like Britain's NHS? For a start, every phase of its evolution has been out of date even as it started. Its founders created a national system in the image of pre-war public medicine. Large public hospitals and the 'panel system' were a way of attacking widespread infectious diseases like tuberculosis, diphtheria and measles. But within a few years of the creation of the NHS, these acute infections had been largely controlled by the introduction of antibiotics and vaccination. We are saddled with this system today, though it is obvious that a better job would be done by a new decentralised system, much more responsive to changing needs.

Without the tug of real customers and all the market intelligence they provide, decisions become 'political'. Hospitals are built to settle favours. More 'political' decisions follow, none of which have much to do with patients, though each one is justified, no doubt, by rhetoric mentioning 'service'. Above all, the public service is 'captured' by the most influential groups within it. Patients, like Mr Benton, determine very little of what is done in the NHS.

William Beveridge himself believed that the demand for medical care would wither away. He thought there was a fixed pool of ill health, which would disappear if medical treatment were freely available.

The assumption is wrong not just because we human beings will always have health problems to worry about, but because public monopoly is a poor way to solve them. With the NHS the public is in a very weak position. The NHS rations health care; patients have to take what they are given. They have no standards of comparison. They can make no significant choices. There is no use of market pricing as a 'discovery procedure', as Frederick Hayek would call it; for an unchallenged monopoly is never able to anticipate the needs of individuals, or to anticipate the advance of knowledge as multiple competitors in a market can. Competition is vital, in medicine as in anything else. Without it there is no incentive to find out a customer's needs and serve them. If a privileged group can stifle competition and control a market, it will. In the NHS that is the doctors. Consequently, the system has been heavily skewed towards their needs. The customers who will do best are the middle classes because they know how to fight the bureaucracy. They have the 'political' skills to write letters or address a personal complaint to the community health council. They take authority in the workplace. They know how to get things done.

In this sad account of the unavoidable effects of a licensed monopoly on a public service, no blame is attached. Nothing is solved by tirades against doctors or any other group. Human beings follow their own interests. If a monopoly power is given, it will be used. If a customer has no clout, a supplier will not do his best. The public authorities end up 'captured' by the people they are supposed to control. If these processes are universal, they undermine some common assumptions about another public monopoly, the state.

*

The 'machinery of state', the 'wheels of government' – these are the analogies that people use about the corporate state and its bureaucracies. A welfare state retains the goals of socialism – a high degree of equality and social justice – but eschews the methods of socialism – massive public ownership, absolute coercion. It adds new tasks to the traditional state duties of defence and the maintenance of order. The modern state sees itself as benign, acting in the public good. Hence the analogy of the machine. Only a machine can dispense fairly without favour or self-interest, only a machine can set itself apart from greedy humanity, acting for that greater good which it must calculate and define as part of its function.

By claiming superhuman powers of cost-benefit analysis, the state justifies its right to coerce individuals, groups and companies, its confiscations of private property, and all its forms of taxes and duties. The state knows better than individuals how to spend money.

In this vision of the modern state, it is rational, doing good in a fair society. It redistributes incomes from the rich to the poor. Images of a modern corporate state are the number-crunching econometric models that make spreadsheets of our future economic prospects, the huge spinning discs that hold the welfare rolls and activate payments to dependent children or students or pensioners, the White Paper that represents the pondered and sifted views of fine minds.

The economic argument for an interventionist state lies in the 'welfare economics' developed by Keynes's teacher, Arthur Cecil Pigou. Economists already knew about 'public goods', – certain things, like defence, which the state has to provide because they are hard to charge to individuals. But Pigou argued that the market was falling so far short of the abstractions of perfection invented by the classical economists that the state had a duty to correct 'externalities' of private exchange. An 'externality' occurs when an open market does not work to the benefit of all. If a lot of people rush to a new oilfield and dig many shallow wells, less oil may be recovered than if the state gives a contract to one extractor. The state should minimise the 'waste' associated with such free-market behaviour. Another flaw was a tendency to monopoly. The discovery of 'market failure' proved to be a huge job-generating opportunity for economists. But if employed by the public, they and other civil servants had to be privy to a special and rarefied form of knowledge named 'the public interest'.

As we have seen, in the first flush of the vision of the modern state Beatrice Webb spoke of the 'unassuming experts' needed to run it. But, forty years on from the elaboration of this theme, are we seeing a new kind of 'externality'? Does the very system designed to defeat the evils of monopoly power and unaccountable might represent an unregulated monopoly greater than any we have seen? Is there a correlation between a large and growing state sector and, say, the sluggish growth rates of Great Britain? Are the shortcomings evident in the NHS reproduced at the level of the state?

People are now asking questions. How does the state perceive the public interest? Is the public interest adequately defined by the political process? And can it be adequately implemented by the administrative machinery of the state? What is the machine? Is there a machine?

A new school of thinkers tries to observe and describe what the servants of the public really do. Public-choice theory is the name given to a school of economic thought that seeks to understand how public, as opposed to private (or 'market'), choice actually operates. Its basic assumption is that the individuals responsible for providing public services and goods are no different from those in the private sector. In other words, they are engaged in the rational pursuit of their own self-interest. The principal theorists of the public-choice school are American, although they are increasingly well represented in the universities of other countries.

Public-choice theorists also look at the way bureaucracies and politicians supply goods to demanding voters. They analyse the failures to provide such goods efficiently, and suggest remedies. They presume that public servants are as fallible and as self-centred as the rest of us, but have special privileges and access to resources. In their vision, the departments of the modern state are like the principalities of a feudal kingdom, owing qualified allegiance to the king or chief executive, jostling for power and degrees of independence. They subject what the 'producers' of state services try to do to critical analysis. The activities of government, whether new regulations, different patterns of taxation, or new welfare benefits, are compared for their relative efficiency, using the tested methods of the market economist.

In other words, the public-choice theorists look inside the machine. What do they see? The machine is just people. Civil servants, officials, manual workers, secretaries – people who except for the nature of their employer have the same aspirations as anyone else. They want to earn more and enjoy better social status. But they are isolated from the major determining forces in society. With few exceptions they work in organisations which are monopoly suppliers. If they were businessmen they would try to increase profits by cutting costs, creating markets, building market shares, improving efficiency and expanding companies. Because they cannot do this, they seek to expand their profit opportunities in other ways.

They seek to maximise their prestige, their power, their opportunities. They seek to increase the size of their departments or their sub-departments, or to improve their working conditions, using their collective power to improve their non-wage benefits. This activity is hard to restrain because there is no competition. Moreover, the NHS, the police, civil servants are all suppliers of important services to government. They know more about their costs than government does. They can offer important 'services' to electorally powerful groups like doctors or farmers but argue that they are vital to the public too. The upshot is that politicians tend to give in to their requests.

They can also seek out 'problems' to be tended by them and their colleagues. Wage benefits are only a small part of the rewards the public sector seeks. One ambition of government agencies is to make more people dependent on their services. Thus a Ministry of Agriculture may devise new research projects, develop a farm policy, think up new regulations and services for farmers, which all enhance its role. Its dependants, the farmers, become clients of the department.

These ideas illuminate other areas. Politicians, seeking votes, can be seen as entrepreneurs seeking support instead of profits. But the markets of politics are blunter and less information-rich than markets sensitive to prices. Price markets respond to individual preferences, political markets to collective preferences, clumsily signalled at election time.

James Buchanan and Gordon Tullock of the Center for Policy Studies at George Mason University in Virginia have done the important job of labelling democracy's defects and economic distortions.[10] Why, for instance, does the system surrender gains to interest groups that clearly make the community worse off? Because the benefits of spending programmes are highly concentrated while the taxes that pay for them are diffused. 'If you stand to get $1000 in benefits you'd be willing to spend a lot of time on the phone to a politician, but he will get no pressure from those who will only pay a penny extra on their tax,' explains James Buchanan.

Opportunity spurs people to make money out of government. Politicians may fall prey to special interest groups who have concentrated their resources to persuade them to legislate to the group's advantage, while the average voter would find such an expenditure of time and effort a waste of time. Commercial interests become what public-choice people call 'rent-seekers'. 'If people sense there's profit to be made from government, they will go where the profit is. If there's a lot of money to be made people will invest heavily.' James Buchanan draws a parallel between lobbyists in Washington and the struggle for import licences in some countries. In a study of competition for import permits in Turkey and India, Anne Kreuger, of the University of Minnesota, shows that the struggle absorbed up to 10 per cent of GNP.[11]

In the term originated by the public-choice theorists, a

government department tends to get 'captured' by the industry it regulates. Bureaucrats get to know the people in the industries they regulate. Their prospects chime together. Bureaucrats move from government to high positions in the industries they know. The Interstate Commerce Commission becomes an agency for the American railroads. These and other defects of the modern welfare state lead Tullock and Buchanan to support tough constitutional limitations which we will look at in another chapter.

In close-up, the welfare state looks more like an interest-group state. Along with the great industrial organisations and their sponsoring departments, there are the labour unions, the employers' lobbies and powerful charities. In Britain, these organisations are even permitted to 'sponsor' Members of Parliament. The institutions are concerned, inevitably, with their own survival, with power and influence and with their growing overheads. The English historian Keith Middlemas describes a corporate Britain run by subtle accords between institutions and interest groups, like the Trades Union Congress, the Confederation of British Industry and the great departments of state.[12] Smaller bodies hover on the periphery of the state system, ready to mobilise effort when they need to. In the brokering that takes place between them, the 'general' or 'public interest' sometimes speaks with a very faint voice indeed.

The modern state has a court: the capital city. Why do the British believe they have the best medical system in the world? Because most patients do not know of a better one and because journalists, officials, commentators and the bureaucrats tell them so. The courtiers are the intellectuals, the journalists, workers in pressure groups or tax-exempt research institutions. They are highly dependent on government and on the information services government provides. Sometimes they depend on the state for their living – working for the universities, advising state organisations. They run publishing houses, television stations, write columns in the newspaper. There are court entertainments to gratify this group along with other leading citizens who are drawn to the capital.

The Arts Council of Great Britain was launched by none other than John Maynard Keynes in 1943. His thinking was conditioned by the radical populism of CEMA, a wartime experiment designed to bring the arts to the people, which used to sponsor concerts in factories. There is a fine old piece of film showing Moura Lympany playing the piano in the Ford factory at Dagenham during a lunch break. In 1943 Keynes described his aims in a radio talk. He said the work of the council should be 'enjoyed'. He thought it should avoid the 'excessive prestige of metropolitan standards and fashions'. And he felt it should be a permanent body, 'independent by constitution'. Today the Arts Council anxiously defends a house ideology of its own devising in which each component – 'excellence', 'national institutions', and the 'arms' length principle' – marks the spot where a basic aim was surrendered. 'Excellence' is its way of dodging the fact that most people do not enjoy what they pay for. To justify its continuing support for unpopular arts, the Council has had to adopt a pretension Keynes avoided. It claims to be a guardian of 'excellence'. 'Independent' it is not. The Arts Minister of the day chooses the chairman of the Council, approves the appointment of the secretary-general, chooses the members of the Council, and gets a personal report from one of his staff on every Council meeting.

'Metropolitan standards' have won the day. The Council's justification for its excessive spending in the south-east of England is that London contains 'national institutions', available to everybody. But it is Londoners who get the lion's share of the benefits. At Covent Garden, where ticket-holders received, in 1981, £12 a visit from the rest of the population, only 14 per cent of the audience comes from outside the home counties. The miner in South Shields is paying for a stockbroker's night out.

In fact, the Council has become a promoter of what Walter

Bagehot called the 'dignified parts' of government. Large amounts of its money are devoted to ornaments of the capital, harmonising its products with those of other ceremonial institutions of the state. The Council is only one of those agencies forming the circlet of rewards that graces those working at the heart of our political system, making it attractive to aspirants from without, satisfying to those within, confirming a right to rule. It promotes life in the capital. 'If', as the sociologist Professor Laurie Taylor put it, 'you say to one social group that your taste is so good we have to provide vast sums of money for you to exercise it, that group really must feel like an elite group in society.'[13] This group confidently defines its urban amusements as the essential culture of the age.

Britain's National Theatre does not have to be 'national' to survive. It survives because it is an ornament of the capital. Our political centre contains both opera-loving City financiers and theatre-loving administrators. The National Theatre puts on 'difficult' plays for left-wing bureaucrats or explores the long tail of the European avant-garde. What the Council cares about, in keeping with other public cultural institutions, like the public broadcasters, is survival. They function in a force field in which they have to accommodate diverse pressures, but most of them come from within the governing elite. The 'public' is out there somewhere, indistinct, like a patient ignored by the health service.

One element which has been identified as inhabiting capital cities has drawn the particular attention of some of the writers whose thoughts we follow in this book. They have been labelled by Irving Kristol in the USA as the 'new class'.[14] They are activists. They work for the public interest, work for others, define the poor and work out ways to help them. They are middle-class and altruistic. They prefer to work with what Marx identified as the 'lumpen proletariat' or urban poor, not the working classes in his meaning of the term. The dependency of the urban poor gives the 'new class' meaning. The intellectual consensus of this class is rationalist. It believes there is an administrative solution to poverty. It wants answers and its stock-in-trade is providing them. Trained in sociology, it places the causes of deviance and poverty within the structure of society.

The 'new class' had an exciting rise to prominence in the USA during the 1960s, the period of the Great Society. Kristol explains their role:

> Politicians are always looking for new ideas, new policies to sell to their public, policies that are attached to their name and which will ensure their re-election. In the post-war years our politicians acquired staffs of bright young aggressive people from universities whose job it was to dream up programmes which no one had ever thought of before. We have therefore produced, in this country, an educated class whose careers are linked to the state. . . . The 'new class' is the educated class that really wants to shift power or influence away from the private sector and towards the government. They would deny indignantly that they were socialists, but nevertheless they want a highly regulated society.

In the United States, the 'new class' is sometimes referred to as the 'knowledge industry'. In the half-century between 1920 and 1972, the number of faculty members at American colleges and universities increased from 48,000 to over 600,000, with a quarter of that growth occurring in a mere five years, between 1965 and 1970. In the view of the writer Michael Novak, 35 per cent of American GNP is 'supplied by the knowledge industry'. Most workers in this industry depend for their livelihood on expanding government expenditure. Most are Democrats. In the 1960s the 'new class' engaged in a kind of status-struggle with the business community. 'New class' members felt the USA had entered a 'post-industrial phase'. They certainly believed they were a generation with new kinds of problem-solving skills. For that reason they flocked to Washington to support and work for the numerous Great Society programmes of the 1960s, which satisfied their commitment to equality and their optimism about improving the condition of the disadvantaged.

The 'new class' helped, in their turn, to define a new, small movement called the neo-conservatives. Irving Kristol again:

> What created doubts for us in the Great Society programmes of Lyndon Johnson was the fact that they were so very ambitious and seemed to have such a utopian vision of human nature. Most of us in the neo-conservative group had come from either working-class or lower-middle-class families. Most of the people who went into the Great Society programmes came from upper-middle-class families, most of them were Harvard graduates. The consequence was that they thought abolishing poverty was easy, that it could be done simply by devising the right programme. They did not understand the incentives that make people react in a certain way.
>
> One notion was that by giving the local communities more control over their own affairs, by politicising them, you would, in effect, motivate them to cease being poor. That is ridiculous. The so-called community action programmes were all taken over by ambitious careerists, ambitious politicians, and that's not the way to motivate people out of poverty. So we were sceptical from the very beginning of the Great Society programme, about the array of policies that were supposed to abolish poverty, reform education, reform all the criminals.
>
> The underlying assumption of the new class was that improving people is easy, that changing people's motivations is easy, that most of the people most of the time are nice, when really most of the people some of the time are nice. In other words, they had a very benign view of human nature. The assumption was that we had reached the stage, particularly by virtue of improvements in psychology and sociology, whereby we could 'manage social change'. Well, it usually works out that social change manages you.

Today the 'new class' in the USA is a diminished group. 'Yuppies' are more talked about today. After the failure of the Carter administration in 1980, some of them left government and went into business. Others have become bureaucrats who go home at 5.30. The ideological zeal of the 'new class' has lessened. But a citizen of any Western democracy will recognise them as the salariat of the welfare state.

On the other side of the 'new class' stands the underclass: the presumptive beneficiaries of their activities, and the victims of their unintended consequences. We have not exhausted the poverty-producing mechanisms of the modern welfare state.

In Britain a developed form of the welfare state has been a pervasive presence in post-war life. We live and breathe it. In the United States, the big welfare push came much later, in the Kennedy–Johnson years, under the name of the Great Society. It had much more of the nature of a one-off experiment, with results that could be examined against a background of earlier experience.

The Great Society programme was very much the product of the 'new class'. It was run by university graduates with a utopian view of the future, a confidence that changing the world was easy and that people were basically nice. They came from middle-class backgrounds at the end of a post-war boom which just went on and on. The urge to do something was focused by growing public guilt about the position of black people in America. Their politics were 'liberal' in the American meaning of the term. They were what others would call social democrats.

The 'new class' was to get the help of the greatest legislator in American history, President Lyndon Baines Johnson. Yet the Great Society programmers failed, because, as Irving Kristol put it, 'they didn't understand poor people'.

A young man called Charles Murray was one of the 'technicians' whose job it was to evaluate the Great Society programmes, identifying those which were the most successful at curing the illnesses of society. Later he was to become the chief evaluator of the Great Society itself, and write up his findings in a remarkable book called *Losing Ground* (1984).[15]

The Great Society was, as he puts it, a 'grab bag' of programmes – Medicaid, job training, 'community action' projects, loans to low-income farmers and businessmen, a domestic Peace Corps, and many, many more. Murray notes that there was an early loss of confidence in the slogan about people 'wanting a hand, not a handout', and in the idea of people bootstrapping themselves up. The programme then became more heavily focused on the redistribution of resources to the poor and disadvantaged. In conversation with us, he explained his findings.

By nearly every measure he chose, he found that the Great Society programmes had not alleviated poverty, but increased it. The exception was help to the aged, one of its 'successes'. Otherwise Murray argues that the large-scale social welfare programmes of the Great Society failed comprehensively in their objectives of decreasing poverty, helping blacks to overcome their special difficulties, and aiding the young people at whom so many programmes were aimed.

He finds that these large-scale expenditures increased poverty, reduced employment, retarded education, increased crime and produced many single-parent families. These claims are lavishly supported with statistics.

Young blacks, for instance, showed a decrease in their chances of getting a job from 1968 when rules governing the labour market changed as a result of Great Society programmes. In an unforeseen consequence of massive proportions, he found that all young people showed an increase in unemployment, particularly pronounced among blacks. In education, the proportion of black students aged between twenty and twenty-four fell each year from 1977, despite continuing increases in loans and grants. There was a drop in the SAT (Scholastic Aptitude Test) scores of US pupils. Crime grew, and its relative impact on the poor worsened. In 1965, assaults on poor whites and middle-class whites were about equal in numbers, at 150 per 100,000 people. Crime rose rapidly in the next fifteen years. Assaults on middle-class whites rose to 910. But the risks of daily life were vastly greater for the poor. By 1979 poor whites were suffering 768 more assaults for every 100,000 persons than middle-class whites, and blacks were suffering 660 more. The greatest human price for rising crime was paid by the poor, both black and white.

Murray argues that a new series of incentives created by the poverty programmes encouraged people to sacrifice their long-term best interest for short-term gains. The programmes made it rational to avoid the sorts of long-term commitments (marriage, steady, low-paid entry-level work, disciplined study) that had traditionally made it possible for the poor to climb the American ladder.

It is Murray's belief that the programmes systematically rewarded the very activities which they were supposed to stop, attacking the whole pattern of incentives that help poor people out of poverty. It was, he says, like 'giving people carrots without any countervailing stick if they didn't behave the way you wanted'. He takes the job programme called CETA, named after the Comprehensive Employment and Training Act. It was designed to socialise people into the market place, helping them to become good employees and hold down a job. But there was no incentive to work hard. 'New entrants might start working hard, but the others would say "Don't do that. If you do that you make it harder for the rest of us." They didn't need to work hard for the money. The whole thing became a "con". There was no reality test.'

But Murray does not wish to imply that being on the dole is fun. 'There's a loss of dignity and pride that you can't get away from, but it just doesn't make sense to behave differently.' And it is not just a question of payments. People do not react blindly to economic stimuli. The moral environment was changing. Illegitimacy among teenagers became acceptable. Historically there have been strong sanctions against girls who conceive out of wedlock in poor communities because of the burden it imposes on society. All that changed. Status values altered dramatically. Getting married, having a wife, holding down a dull job becomes a degrading thing to do. And the welfare structure both reflected and supported that change.

Aid to poor people was meant to help them out of the cycle of poverty. But Murray argues that by, as it were, improving poverty, it did the opposite, perpetuating the conditions that make people poor. For instance, there was a large increase in the number of single-parent families. 'In 1960 a girl who got pregnant would either have to persuade the boy to marry her or give up the child for adoption. By 1970 she could just about get along. The boy could now live with her without any loss of benefit, which would have been impossible in the 60s.'

The Great Society years revised attitudes about how to treat problem children in school. 'You quit kicking out the kids that made trouble, stopped corporal punishment, stopped demanding academic standards for which kids hadn't been prepared by their parents. The grading system was changed because we didn't want to show some kids failing when it wasn't their fault. Whole classes were disrupted.'

Murray is dismissive of the view that some pathological children are involuntarily involved in criminal behaviour. 'If you are a youngster who is only getting arrested for one out of every ten crimes you commit, and if you go on probation again and again (in Chicago the average number of probations before imprisonment is thirteen) you don't have to look on that kid as pathologically evil. He's just a kid trying to perceive the way the world works.'

As Murray constantly reminds us, it is the ordinary youngster who should be considered when we assess the impact of the Great Society programmes. 'The ordinary youngster who's been plugging away doing the right thing, looks over his shoulder and sees the guy next to him who's been in trouble with juvenile court, or had a drug problem, or been kicked out of school gets the first slot on the job programme. If he sees a kid who's loused up all sorts of things getting ahead, he's going to ask: "Why am I doing this? Why am I behaving this way?"'

Murray associates the Great Society with a 'new class' of intellectuals, as does Irving Kristol. They accepted the view that poverty was a result of structural defects in the economy. But they showed a failure to understand the mechanisms that raise poor people from poverty. 'They did not accept the meaning and use of pain. Part of growing up', says Murray, is 'learning that actions have consequences'. 'People try to do good without pain, but pain has its uses.' While young people are 'at their most flexible, while they are strongest, we should show them that actions have consequences. Do not subsidize their errors or praise their mistakes.'

Charles Murray now says he would be 'ninety per cent happy' if 'the US could go back to the 50s and pick up their social programmes from there'. In his view, the way to help poor people is first, and above all, to make people safe in the poorer communities. He puts much poverty down to the crime levels that stop 'good people getting on'. He would like poor people to get the schools that they want, 'orderly schools that teach the basics'. Above all he would hope that we accept that government does not know how to 'do good by giving people things'. The state does not know how to give people things in the right way, he says. Giving is best left to private people. Indeed, in the USA there is growing evidence that charitable giving outdoes public giving in dollars received by the poor because of the way bureaucracies soak up resources.

After sixteen years of watching public assistance programmes, Murray believes he has observed the production of poverty and the creation of dependency. And dependency and poverty promote each other. Murray now thinks the state should cut all welfare to the able-bodied young on the grounds that he sees no way of giving a government safety-net that does not act as a perverse incentive.

The Great Society, Murray believes, prevented the poor from developing their resources, developing what Adam Smith called the 'patrimony of the poor': 'The patrimony of a poor man lies in the strength and dexterity of his hands; and to hinder him from employing this strength and dexterity in what manner he thinks proper is a plain violation of this most sacred property.'

In Britain there are towns, like Sunderland, which are almost completely dependent on subsidies. Sunderland is in the North of England, a region of three million people, which ranks tenth from the bottom (measured in terms of income per person) of 130 EEC regions. Since 1979 £2.3 billion has been spent in this region by government in development grants and other aid. The region also received money from the EEC. In spite of this, it has lost 240,000 jobs since 1977. It has fewer self-employed people than any other region. Social security payments for the region are 42 per cent higher than the British average.

In the centre of Sunderland stands the civic centre, an expensive building, cleverly designed in two hexagons. Down the road, past the labour exchange and next to the empty dockyards, are the council estates of the East End. Round the corner stand rows of empty, new industrial units with ill-fitting doors. The EEC Development Fund's logo is displayed on their fronts.

Half the working population of Sunderland is employed in the public sector. Over half the population live in council-owned houses. Less than 10 per cent of school-leavers go on to any form of higher education. Yet in 1985 under 9 per cent of the sixteen-year-old school-leavers who left in July had a job by December. Few people are employed in small firms, and business start-ups have a high failure rate. In places like the Downhill Estate in Sunderland, over 80 per cent of the residents are dependent on supplementary benefit. They are depressed. They are dependent. The planning blight of Sunderland is immobility. The British welfare state cannot deliver the 'mild and provident care' that socialism promised. It cannot bring the world's ships to the yards of Sunderland. It cannot have the world's steel made at the giant mills of Redcar. It cannot make the people of Sunderland rich without a transfer of revenue that would bring the nation to a standstill. Faced with Sunderland, its ideas run out.

*

The arguments expressed in this chapter are blunt. A welfare state that creates national monopolies to provide services to its people will create institutions that give a poor and declining service to the public, favouring the strong against the weak. It will destroy the very habits and institutions that raise the poor from poverty and make all people productive and free. The welfare state, by enlarging the sphere of government, enlarges the sphere of 'political' decision-making. Decisions made in the political sphere are likely to be prompted by the interests of particular groups and not by the general good. Institutions of the welfare state, like huge nationalised industries or council estates, immobilise the dependent poor. The only satisfaction they can offer is to those whose careers and salaries are a function of the dependency of others.

Faced with Sunderland, we see that the promise of the welfare state was written on water. That promise was that it would look after people, but it has been unable to prepare a future for them. Its 'discovery procedures' do not work. It disengages the mechanisms by which people defeat poverty, and leaves the poor stranded.

3
Human Capital

A friend to all is a friend to none.

Aristotle

Gary Becker and Thomas Sowell are two people who became interested in why different groups of people progress at different rates and in different ways. They both realised that physical capital (industrial might and a high standard of living) was an inadequate explanation of why some groups get ahead. In their different ways they began to work with the notion of intangible benefits, refining that down to the notion of 'human capital', the mysterious and productive accumulation of skills and hidden learning that parents pass on to their children. It is our values, our motivation. It is the way we meet a crisis or say goodbye, the way we handle money or talk to a policeman. It is our culture and all our knowledge, our habits and our skills.

In the United States, in the mid-1960s, the 'new class' went on a whistle-stop tour round the main inequities of American life. The train carried a banner portraying the sainted face of John Kennedy. The engineer was Lyndon Johnson. But there were dissidents. They shared the objectives but were uncomfortable with the rhetoric, and with the radical glow of the civil rights campaign. But so powerful was the momentum of the civil rights movement that the dissidents felt they had to get to grips with the issues it raised.

Gary Becker's first project as a postgraduate student in the civil rights era was to try to find a way to measure the 'prejudice' of white employers. Where he found that black workers with similar skills and qualifications to whites had to accept less money for doing the same job, he would take that

This chapter is based on conversations with Gary Becker, Anne Wortham, Walter Williams, Ed Snider, Tibor Machan, Irving Kristol and Frederick Hayek.[1]

as a 'measure' of white prejudice. His thinking then turned over. If black people were willing to take lower wages, because of prejudice, that implied that some employers might be losing out by not hiring blacks at all. Their prejudice was costing them money. Was there somewhere in here a mechanism for undermining prejudice?

For instance, the white employer who did hire blacks would gain a competitive edge on the one who did not. By reducing his costs of production, he would prosper. And by living and working close to black people, he should get to like them better and lose his 'prejudice'. Was the market, therefore, colour blind? If this analysis is right, it could mean that minimum wage laws, passed specially to stop employers paying less for whites than for blacks, were a disaster. A prejudiced employer who had to pay the same for whites and blacks would obviously hire whites. Could this be another case of unintended consequences? Did some anti-discrimination laws, like some of the anti-poverty programmes, have an effect the reverse of what was intended?

Gary Becker, who is now an economics professor at the University of Chicago, does not condone prejudice, but nor does he believe that you can eradicate it by a law or a lecture. He prefers to take the economist's path, treating prejudices as 'preferences'. We should expect to have to pay for our preferences, and we give them up if they get too expensive. People express their preferences in the decisions that they take. These preferences may be undesirable. We may look down on them. We cannot erase them. Social policy may be used to make undesirable preferences (like smoking) even more expensive and unattractive, but policy-makers should be cautious about unanticipated effects.

The idea of 'human capital' seems to go back at least as far as the English economist Alfred Marshall. It was revived after the Second World War to help explain the extraordinarily fast recovery of Western Europe. It means the skills from which we can gain an economic return. The Germans, for example, lost much of their physical capital in the war, but those who survived retained their human capital and helped the country to achieve a rapid recovery. Gary Becker applied the idea to the question why students stay on in college rather than take highly paid jobs. He found that it was easily explained by the extra wages they would earn in later life. In other words, the temporary sacrifice of earnings was an economically rational decision, not unlike a firm's decision to plough back its profits, a worthwhile investment in the improvement of skills, knowledge and life-chances. A society in which the production of human capital works well will be better off than one in which it is sporadic.

Becker developed the idea into a general approach to human decisions, in particular to decisions inside the family because this is when, he believes, the habit of building up human capital is generated.[2] His theory applies the tests of economics to ordinary behaviour to see if human beings are rational, if they act in ways that improve their 'utility' or worth. It deals with the investments, the skills and the productivity of human beings. If the behaviour of students could be explained by rational choice, what else? What about love, child-bearing, the family? It is Becker's examination of the choices that families make which has made his work so important.

The family is one of the fundamental organisms of society. It largely determines the respective roles of men and women. It makes decisions about the education of children and about the rate of growth of the population. One may assume that men and women make rational decisions about whom they should marry, when they should marry, how many children they should have, and how they should spend their money. One may also assume that if public policy changes the pattern of incentives, rational, self-interested individuals will respond in new ways and make new choices about child-rearing and marriage. These changes may have good or bad social effects. Understanding the 'rationality' of the family is therefore important. If Becker can show that families make rational and good decisions, he is making a case for leaving the family free from interference.

> Parents, while their children are young, teach them, influence their morals, they affect their learning while in school. If one believed that people were fundamentally irrational, that they made foolish decisions, that they were highly influenced by the last person who tried to persuade them to do this or that, the case for giving these individuals the freedom would be much weaker. So I think there has to be a close connection between the belief in free choice and a belief that, on average, people will use these choices in a wise way.

What does the human capital approach do about the emotions – about love, anger, fear? It cannot expect to understand them the way a psychologist would. It has to accept them as 'givens'. It then looks for a working definition of each. Love, say the human capital theorists, is 'caring about someone'. 'In a rational framework we define love as caring about an individual. It is not irrational, if I love somebody, to risk my life. I compare the consequences of my child drowning and see that would be terrible for me, and so I risk my life.' It is also rational to 'economise' your love, trying to get the maximum 'utility' out of it. Or you can figure out how to win the maximum 'return' on your love from someone else.

Becker argues that many changes in the behaviour of the family are rational and follow the economic changes of the last thirty years. There has, for instance, been a huge increase in the employment of women. This means that as a woman's time becomes more valuable, the cost of time spent raising a child goes up. The cost of anything includes the 'opportunity cost', the other uses of that time which have been foregone. Research in the USA now estimates that 70 per cent of the costs of a child are the foregone wages of a woman. This kind of analysis predicts that women would be increasingly reluctant to raise children. The birth rate has certainly fallen. And, as the labour-force participation of women goes up, the 'value' of marriage goes down. In the past women gave up the whole of their productive lives to raise children. The wife got a promise of total support in return; she had no means of supporting herself. Now that this drastic division of labour has weakened, the marriage tie is weakening with it.

But there are limits to the rationality of role-sharing. Although many women go out to work, they may still prefer part-time work and flexibility in return for lower wages. They work a 'twilight shift' when husband is home, or turn up late on Wednesdays when they have a school run. An economist would predict that in return for this extra flexibility or 'utility', women would settle for earnings lower than men's. Equal pay legislation has, in fact, had only a modest impact on women's wages in the lower reaches of the labour market.

Becker concludes that the family is a highly efficient division of labour, which wife and husband jointly undertake in order to make themselves a more productive pair. This division of labour, less sharp than in the past, is surviving, and it is not necessarily at the expense of women. In a division of labour everyone gains from the other workers' experience and specialisations. If a man specialises in the market place, it could be because he is more skilled there. If a woman specialises in household activities, it could be because this is where she excels. Both profit. The total earnings of women go up as well as those of men. It has advantages to both sides. Says Becker: 'The fact that we observe the sharp sexual division of labour throughout history is not accident or simply a result of exploitation. This doesn't mean that there is no discrimination against women – but it is not the explanation for the division of labour common to all societies.'

The lack of impact of the feminist movement on the lives of ordinary families may find an explanation here. Most feminist writers and campaigners are professional or career women. They expect to earn as much as men, and they probably do; for research shows no sex differences in pay at the upper echelons of professional work. Non-professional working women may, however, have a different perception of work, seeing it as a family supplement. Although the proportion of women at work in the USA with children below the age of six rose from below 20 per cent in 1960 to 42 per cent by 1980, these working women show a dramatic disloyalty to the labour market. They are eleven times as likely as men to leave the workforce voluntarily and their work effort declines rapidly as family income goes up. The feminists may have misjudged popular feeling.

The altruism expressed within the family is belittled by some as 'selfish', inferior to the true altruism expressed in a concern for the wellbeing of your fellow men. A human capital theorist sees things differently. Altruism is a fact, a given. We might define it as the 'wish to put someone else's interest first'. Even if its sources are not 'rational', we still want to get the maximum 'utility' out of it. Altruism is a sacrifice of yourself, something on which you spend time, maybe the whole of your life. It achieves its greatest effect by concentration. Its 'utility' is wasted if it is spread too far. Personal altruism is also much better informed about its objects than a general altruism could be. 'Altruism gets very weak as you go beyond the family,' argues Becker.

> It is very hard to be altruistic to a large number of individuals, because altruism means by definition that a person is willing to spend their life or energy for others. But they only have a limited amount of it. If they're spending a tiny bit on hundreds of people, it will have very little influence on any one of them. And again, if I'm being altruistic towards hundreds, you, as a recipient, won't be much concerned about my altruism, because you're not gaining much from me and you won't hesitate very much to harm me. . . . Altruism is of much more value in the family. Outside the family a selfish framework is a more powerful framework for understanding behaviour.

Sometimes altruism in families goes wrong. Parents exploit their children under the guise of altruism, grooming them for ballet schools, or pushing them through academic hoops that they cannot manage. With these small exceptions, Becker shows that the human family is a highly efficient institution. In the modern world an altruistic family need not follow the 'nuclear' pattern in which dad goes out to work while mum looks after children. A highly paid woman may find it worth her while to hire a mother's help. A woman has the same right as a man to pursue her own interests. The family is not only efficient. If Becker's analysis is correct, it is a key institution in the avoidance of poverty. Its division of labour is expert and highly productive. It focuses altruism and love for others in a way no other institution can. It determines the quality of the next generation. Becker's very success in showing how efficiently the family nurtures human capital and passes it on suggests that public programmes could have destructive effects, especially if they weaken the two-person family.

> Young women who have had babies have their lives affected for a long period of time. Often they drop out of school, so this affects their education and their earning power. Having a baby also affects one's earning power if there is no one to look after the baby. People who have had children at an early age find it hard to marry. Marriages are less stable. These can be serious consequences.

Does that lead Becker to take a tough 'old-fashioned' position on, say, divorce? No, but it follows from his argument that a single-parent family, with none of the benefits of a division of labour, is inefficient, and that the recent rise in the rate of teenage illegitimacy among poor communities in the United States will deepen their poverty and diminish their ability to preserve human capital. Human capital, like physical capital, leads to a stream of future income or wealth.

Divorce may be better than a miserable marriage, but if legislation has a destructive effect on the family, it is wrong, says Becker. In poor single-parent families, the learning rate of children is likely to be slow. Moreover, if public policy directed at the poor has the specific effect of destabilising the family, then the poor will suffer disproportionately from it. In the

USA poor often means black, where single family heads are now the norm. Becker and Charles Murray agree. Great Society legislation caused the break-up of many black families.

In the 1960s, the 'bourgeois marriage' was derided. It was fashionable to admire 'extended' families. Today some New Enlightenment thinkers are working hard to revive the dignity and standing of the dual role of man and wife. 'Women have long horizons within their bodies, glimpses of eternity sited in their wombs,' writes George Gilder. 'Civilized society is dependent upon the submission of the short-term sexuality of young men to the extended maternal horizons of women. . . . The woman gives [a man] a unique link with the future and a vision of it; he gives her faithfulness and a commitment to a lifetime of hard work. If work effort is the first principle of overcoming poverty, marriage is the other prime source of upwardly mobile work.'[3]

In March 1965 Daniel Patrick Moynihan, currently Senator for New York, became the first person to signal publicly his disquiet at the break-up of the black family. He argued that half the black population suffered from a 'social pathology' whose source was the broken family where husbands deserted wives and children in distressingly large numbers. Anti-poverty legislation and bad social policy were speeding the break-up. Moynihan, like Charles Murray, is concerned about the perverse incentives created by Great Society programmes, such as jobs programmes and aid for parents of dependent children. The theory of 'moral hazard' holds that if you subsidise something – whether it is single parenthood or lack of work effort – you will get more of it. Charles Murray draws the following little scenario, one of many, in *Losing Ground*.

Harold and Phyllis have been going together for a while and Phyllis has become pregnant. In 1960, says Murray, they would probably have married and he would have taken a low-income job that might eventually have led to something better. In 1979, however, the Aid For Dependent Children Programme gives Phyllis an income as large as that which

Harold could earn, yet if she were to marry him she would lose that. If they live together, Harold's income will supplement the AFDC grant, as long as they remain single. Harold will get work, if he can, but it will not be so important for the 1970 Harold to remain in a tedious entry-level job as it would have been for the 1960 Harold. He can get unemployment insurance between jobs, and in any case Phyllis's AFDC grant will let them get by even without that. Harold has missed the chance to build up a steady employment record. The couple are likely to break up.[4]

The last twenty years has been especially bad for black men in the USA. In the period between 1940 and 1960 the average black wage moved from between 40 and 50 per cent of a white wage to 75 per cent. Since then it has fallen away badly, although black women have almost reached parity with whites. Becker attributes this decline in the progress of black families to the effect of social policy on black people, leading to the destruction of the black family, and the increase of the indigent poor.

America's black citizens had urbanised late into a de-industrialising America. Their cultural disadvantages were great. They had faced shameful prejudice and hostility. Yet in the twenty years after 1940 the urban black family had established itself. There was a period of prosperity and growth, though that process was far from complete when the civil rights era was reached. There were still many black poor, who then became the victims of bad social policy. The unintended consequences of the policy were the deepening poverty of the black underclass, and a reversal of the beneficent post-war trend.

Naturally this is not solely a black problem. The effects of bad social programmes affect white and black, and have the same results everywhere. In Britain British doctors began to report that teenage girls were becoming pregnant in order to receive council accommodation. They became known as the 'gymslip mums'. The council's housing waiting list can be jumped by young mothers. Madge Campbell had her first child ten years ago while living with her mother. She was then able to apply for a council house, as her mother's house was technically overcrowded. Since then she has had a second child, who is now four. Her present benefit amounts to £40.15 a week, after paying fuel bills which are a flat £14 a week. The two-bedroom flat is provided free by the council. When decoration is required she applies for a social security grant to finance it. In Britain the number of single-parent families rose from a steady half million through the 1960s, to just under a million today. Today, Madge Campbell regrets what happened to her.

People like to feel that some things are theirs. 'Me' means nothing if I cannot be sure that some boundary defines what is 'me' and what is 'not me'. My 'property rights' protect this 'me'. People make sure that they get good value out of their own property, but they will not look after other people's so well. A free exchange of goods based on clear property rights gives people an incentive to improve their assets and with it the nation's stock of capital. Parents treat their children a bit like property. The 'selfish' model of human capital economics defines a way in which human capital is improved and conserved. We know of no better. There have in the past been times when this was taken for granted and embodied in popular morality. Prudence was once regarded as a cardinal virtue. Then in the nineteenth century it became something that one exercised automatically, a dull animal habit. The dull habit of prudence may have been underrated.

The struggle to develop and conserve human capital is powerful among immigrants in a new country, and especially powerful when helped by a culture with strong family traditions. Mohinder Singh put both his sons through Bradford Grammar School, an independent fee-paying school. He says: 'If we work together, we can achieve any goal.' His wife, Khasmir, never took a job. 'She ruled the family by love.' Singh has spent much of his working life as a bus conductor; now he is an accounts clerk. He and his wife never go out; they have foregone holidays. He has never been back to India. 'Education', he says, 'is worth a million pounds.' His son

Kanwaljid is in his third year at university and his brother Havinder is soon to join him.

Not far away is the Dudley Hill Post Office, run by Philip and Joyce Cordingley. They too sent their children to Bradford Grammar School. They wanted the best for their children. Philip says the most important things in life are the 'intangibles', the memories that remain with you at the end of your life. He reckons he has the oldest car of all the Bradford parents. Men and women are linked to the future through their children.

Anne Wortham was a black student at Tuskegee Institute in Alabama at the beginning of the civil rights movement. Tuskegee was a segregated college. She supported the civil rights movement because she thought that black people had a unique responsibility to affirm and reassert the civil rights of all Americans.

When Martin Luther King came to her college she realised she was out of step.

> I was frightened by the meeting. The pressure on you as a college student to show your good faith by participating in a march or attending a rally was very great and I didn't like the way I felt in those meetings. Political principles were being discussed as though they were tenets of the sermon on the mount. King was able, as a minister, as a man of God, to bring moral force to these political demands and energise people in a way that they actually took leave of themselves in this auditorium and became one big crowd.

Later she rejected the 'black power' orientation that King began to take. 'It meant that whites were not just wayward and needed saving. They were part of a *system* that was evil.'

Anne Wortham could not accept that capitalism was inherently racist. She describes herself as belonging to the derided black liberal tradition of Booker T. Washington, not the black socialist tradition of W. E. B. Dubois. Nor could she support 'affirmative rights', which she felt led blacks into a 'cynical game'. 'Black rights' were, in her view, 'another name for black privileges', which violated the rights of others. To justify them, blacks had to emphasise their disadvantages, leading them to a 'collectivist' posture where 'I need to know what I can get on the basis of being black'. That 'robs you of a sense of self as a creative force in the world, you just become a category'. She found that posture humiliating.

In this she echoes the thoughts of other black civil rights dissidents, like Walter Williams, now an economics professor at George Frazer University in Virginia, who opposes the practice of integrating schools by bussing children out of their home neighbourhood. 'Bussing is a racial insult. What people are saying is that the only way for there to be black academic excellence is for black people to go and catch a white kid to sit beside.'

Bussing has actually been a comprehensive failure. It has been associated with a drop in standards and 'white flight' from city schools. Walter Williams speaks scathingly about the irrelevance of the programme.

> There is no evidence to suggest that bussing is a means for academic achievement. . . . You go to the many parochial schools or the 400 independent schools and you can see academic excellence occurring. Now the unique feature of this is that they are not accomplishing this through bussing. They are accomplishing this by having kids come to school sober, leaving their guns and their knives home, by teachers that can read and write themselves and parents who are willing to make sure that the kids come to school and do their homework. Black kids need the same thing for academic excellence as white kids . . . a good attitude, parents who care, and teachers who can do the job.

Warren Brookes is a black high-school teacher in Boston whom we talked to. 'It doesn't matter what the colour of the kid sitting next to a student is.' It matters, however, for other purposes. It was for a vision of social justice and how to acquire it that, in 1973, Federal District Judge Arthur W.

Garrity Jr caused the school system of Boston, Massachusetts, to be integrated by forced bussing. At that time there was de facto segregation in most of Boston: children went to neighbourhood schools, and most neighbourhoods were either white or black.

Judge Garrity drew up a plan that divided the city into 'geocodes'. Every parent of a child in the school system had to accept the assignment of their children to 'mixed' schools on the basis of this plan. But the law of unanticipated consequences intervened. The schools did not become integrated. Instead the parents of over half of the white children – and even many of the black parents – put their children in private schools. The result was that ten years after the plan was implemented the percentage of white children in the Boston public schools had fallen from 57 per cent to only 27 per cent: black children were being bussed across town from black neighbourhoods to white neighbourhoods where they attended mostly black schools.

The effects of forced bussing were not just the failure to achieve integrated schools: there were also some very negative consequences. Warren Brookes's own daughter was in her last year of high school when bussing began. Her mother remembers those days with undiminished passion. 'I saw my daughter hit with golf clubs by whites at the school where she was sent. I was sitting there and there was nothing I could do. Bussing has just made the children more aware of colour. My daughter went to school with whites all her life, but it wasn't until bussing started that she was ever called a "nigger".'

The experience of the Brookes reinforces Hayek's point about the value of allowing individuals to make their own decisions. Warren Brookes's daughter's personal liberty was violated. She was prohibited from making the most of her opportunities and forced to act in accordance with a general plan. An individual's own information is so much richer than that of any authority. The Brookes's daughter, for example, was doing fine in the school she was attending when bussing came. Her parents wanted her to stay there; but there was nothing they could do to protect her. A decision had been made on her behalf by a remote authority, a decision that was information-poor. A generation of children all over America have had their lives disrupted by a well-intentioned attempt to take responsibility away from the family, and lodge it with the superior wisdom of governmental authority.

Black people like Anne Wortham and Walter Williams are in support of the constitutional aims of the civil rights movement such as the right to vote but totally opposed to its later search for 'economic justice'. They have become some of the most damning critics of anti-discrimination and welfare policy. One of the most articulate of these critics is the black economist Thomas Sowell of the Hoover Institution. He questions transfers that reduce the 'extent to which those with human capital can afford to have offspring and increase the extent to which those lacking human capital can afford to have offspring'. He notes that studies of the effects of civil rights policy find that the main improvement was in the wages of highly qualified blacks, while unemployment has risen and wages have been depressed among the poorly qualified. He attacked the quota system on the grounds that quotas and other anti-discrimination employment laws made employers afraid to hire young black workers who might not succeed in their work; the employers were afraid that they would be accused of breaking the law when they fired them. Instead they hired advantaged blacks, older people with a track record, thus making it much harder for young blacks to get jobs.

By 1980, college-educated black couples were actually earning more than white couples. Sowell concludes that the net effect of affirmative action, equal opportunity laws and anti-racist legislation is to have made the ostensible beneficiaries worse off. They are just some of the 'many social programs in which, in the *name* of the poor and disadvantaged, those who were already well off were made better off'. Or, as Walter Williams puts it more polemically: 'Affirmative action does nothing for that kid standing out on the street corner in Harlem, shooting up his arm with dope. It does nothing for the 40 per cent of black teenagers in the United States that come out of our schools functionally illiterate, according to a recent study. What is being done with affirmative action is that the names of poor blacks are being invoked as a means for middle-class blacks, or upper-middle-class blacks, to exploit the government programmes in order to make gains for themselves.'

But Sowell has also gone much further. He has argued that the problems of black people are not now the effects of discrimination. Discrimination, in his view, explains very little about the present situation.

All over the world the Chinese have achieved success in the face of horrific and persistent discrimination. Host countries in which they have performed a valuable and wealth-creating role have seldom shown themselves grateful or kind. Slaughter and banishment are persistent events in the history of the overseas Chinese. Yet throughout recent history you can find comments like this one. It comes from a seventeenth-century Catholic priest working in what is now Indonesia:

> Since the Chinese are industrious and clever, they are of the greatest value at Batavia and without their help it would be difficult to live at all comfortably. They cultivate the land; there are scarcely any artisans except Chinese; in a word they are nearly everything.[5]

Right up until the twentieth century the Chinese did not enjoy free and equal status in Indonesia. They could not live outside designated areas or travel freely. Yet they remained a 'perfect type of quiet citizen', noted for industry, frugality and reliability. In post-independence Indonesia, discrimination began again. Chinese newspapers and magazines were banned. Chinese-owned rice mills were confiscated. Race riots rocked Java in 1980, after which President Suharto, though opposed to the rioting, warned the Chinese not to 'demonstrate an attitude and lifestyle that may offend the surrounding larger community'. This story of Chinese success in the face of discrimination is repeated in many countries.

In the United States itself there are cases of extraordinary cultural resilience. The Japanese in America faced terrific discrimination. For long periods they were not allowed to own land and could not become citizens. During the war they lost property and were interned. Yet they are now the most prosperous, most highly paid and best-educated group in the United States. Jews are another group which has achieved a phenomenal success from humble beginnings, and in the face of widely expressed prejudice.

A strange patchwork of success and failure could be made of the various experiences of different racial groups in America. Although black people, as a whole, are still relatively unsuccessful, these aggregates contain a wide scale of differences. Another group of black people, from the West Indies, is one of the most successful minority groups in New York State. Your taxi driver is more likely to come from Jamaica than Harlem. Sowell even turns up some research which shows that blacks who are the descendants of 'free persons of colour' still do better than the descendants of slaves.[6] The Irish in America have done well in politics but not in business. Daniel Boone pioneers and log-cabin builders were usually Scottish or Irish. They were not inclined to tame the wilderness, but kept moving on, giving way to Germans who domesticated the land and built farms. These industrious and careful farmers lived 'much better' than other Americans, and were less 'addicted to the use of spiritous liquors'.

The civil rights movement generated important currents of post-war US social policy. Its enduring effect was to reaffirm the constitutional rights of every US citizen. But it also led to policy decisions and a climate of thinking that were foreign to previous American experience. The civil rights vision was that 'statistical' disparities in income, occupation or education were moral inequities, caused by 'society'. In particular, they were caused by discrimination based on a belief that a particular racial or social group is inferior. The way to remedy these structural inadequacies was through political action.

Since discrimination and failure are not clearly related, the vision is questionable. It became clear to Sowell that different cultures perform differently. Some groups have resilience and wealth-creating power. Others do not. Cultures can learn new skills, but the processes of acculturation are mysterious. Equally mysterious is the transmission of the really useful knowledge called human capital.

Sowell goes further. Political action is *not* the solution to black people's problems. On the contrary political solutions to complex social problems are usually divisive. Measures meant to integrate in fact disintegrate the community. In Sowell's view,

> The politicization of economic and social life increases the costs of intergroup differences, and tends to heighten hostility. . . . Politics offer 'free' benefits for groups to fight over. Markets put prices on benefits, forcing each group to limit its own use of them, thereby in effect sharing with others. A society with both Buddhist and Islamic citizens must somehow allocate its building materials in such a way as to have these materials shared in the building of temples and mosques. If the building materials are shared through economic processes, each set of followers weighs costs against benefits and limits its demand accordingly. But if these same buildings are provided free or otherwise shared through the political process, each group has an incentive to demand the lion's share.

Consensus is very hard to achieve in a society. Where there are differences in values, the costs of political consensus are high and often include bloodshed. A society that limits the need for consensus, limits the danger that it will fall apart. 'Minimizing the need for consensus is one of the advantages of economic processes over political processes.'[7]

In Sowell's account, the weaknesses of the black cultural heritage go back to slavery. De Tocqueville noted, in the 1830s, that the 'colonies in which there were no slaves became more populous and more prosperous than those in which slavery flourished'. Travelling down the Ohio river between the slave state of Kentucky and the free state of Ohio he found the white population 'ignorant and apathetic' on one side and full of 'activity and intelligence' on the other. Slavery left its imprint on white as well as on black. Work habits continued to reflect the resistance to work, the evasion of work, that developed under slavery. In this century, after their huge and recent migration to the north, black people moved into the urban economy without the skills or the traditions for it.

After the war the urban black family established itself and black income rose. The trajectory was broken. Blacks received a setback. The setback came from bad and meddlesome, although well-intentioned, legislation at a time when all that black people needed were their human rights under the constitution. The policies of the 1960s ignored an obvious truth: 'The idea – essentially that obstacles and problems elicit motivation and creativity and impel progress – defies all the canons of current sociology. But the opposite idea – that the stresses of poverty and the provider role, the obstacles and challenges of life, thwart effort and achievement – defies all the experience of history, most especially the history of ethnic groups in America.'[8]

Becker and Sowell tell us to leave people alone. Human systems work. Leave people free to apply their rationality. Insist that they get the right to do that. Allow no other group to interfere. Humans have their own ways and means of betterment.

The moral basis of the New Enlightenment is the idea of 'natural rights'. The notion of natural rights certainly goes back to Roman law and medieval jurisprudence. Some philosophers have been disturbed by the idea that men and women have rights against the state. One of them was Thomas Hobbes. Hobbes's was a brutal and anarchic vision of all-out competition. Man, he finds, is an anti-social animal, a self-aggrandiser and a power-seeker. Men are natural enemies of one another. Dutiful submission to an absolute authority was needed to tame them. Hobbes's philosophy was that of an arch-conservative responding to some disturbing 'rights talk' at the time of the English Civil War.

The modern idea of liberal rights appears with John Locke. There we have the cluster of rights – the right to personal safety and the protection of your property, the obligation of the state to defend its subject, the stability of contracts – which inspired the US Constitution and which still inspire liberals today as the correct description of the limits and responsibilities of government. Natural rights are negative rights. They tell other people to abstain from certain kinds of actions towards you. Locke's theory of rights is rooted in the growth of religious dissent. The 'moral space' that free people occupy today was opened up by English dissenters fighting to delete from the law of the land any public reference to their beliefs.

In the twentieth century the idea of natural rights has been inverted. Social democracy and Marxism have invented other 'positive' rights – the right to a fair wage, the right to a roof over your head, the right to avoid hardship, the right to read, the right to a holiday. These are corruptions of the original concept of rights, which can be summarised in Immanuel Kant's injunction that we treat every person as an end in himself, and not as a means to someone else's. Positive rights represent an attempt to put benefits on the political agendas of societies where the language of politics has traditionally been a language of negative or natural rights.

Present-day social democrats follow thinkers like John Rawls and Ronald Dworkin. Rawls starts by inviting us to imagine ourselves in a state of nature, asking what sort of society we would like if we could choose the society but not our position in it. We would therefore run the risk of being very poor. In his considered view, we would choose a society in which the rich are allowed to be rich only if they make the poor better off in the process. Rawls thinks of wealth as socially produced. If the wealth holdings of an individual appear to have no social value, they can be taken away to be used for public purposes.

Modern libertarian philosophers, like Tibor Machan, however, argue for negative rights only. If we have something which we acquired justly, no one can take it away. We are born with no fundamental duties to the rest of society. His approach to rights, however, assumes that we live our lives in common, and make choices that affect other people. Duties come from these. If you decide to have a child, then you owe duties to that child. If you join a club, you have to pay your fees. But you do not have to join the club and you do not have to become a parent. Human beings are moral agents, needing a space to make decisions from which duties flow. In that space you do good by choice, self-motivated and free. In fact you can only be said to be 'doing good' if you do so free from compulsion.

The philosophy of natural rights leads to a morality of restraints or bans rather than permissions. It defines what people should not do to each other. Its thrust is that other people, individually or corporately, should offer as little interference with *your* life as possible. The most detailed investigation of the political implications of natural rights theory in recent times has been made by the American philosopher Robert Nozick. Nozick argues with the social democratic idea that a fair distribution should be made the guiding principle of a fair society. His mission is to prove that 'no end-state principle or distributional patterned principle of justice can be continuously realized without continuous interference with people's lives.'[9] In other words, no system of social democracy, however enlightened or mild, can fail to infringe natural rights. This illustration of the point is adapted from him.[10]

Let us suppose that, by skilled manipulation, a group of socialist administrators have achieved a 'fair distribution' of wealth. This need not mean that everyone is earning the same amount. It might mean 'fair' by some new sophisticated standard of comparability. It might even follow the definition of 'fairness' developed by Nozick's fellow philosopher John Rawls. (Rawls says that a distribution might be seen as 'fair' if the least well-off group in society would not be made better off by changing it.) Setting aside all the problems of defining this pattern of distribution, we assume it has been done – when along comes Diego Maradona, the great Argentinian footballer, with this offer for Tottenham Hotspur. Maradona is willing to sign a contract with Tottenham Hotspur which stipulates that at each home game £1 of the total ticket price goes directly to him. Spurs supporters contentedly drop a £1 coin into a box marked 'Maradona' on their way into the ground, and Maradona takes the contents home after every game. The season starts. The club does well. People cheerfully pay the extra money to see the great Maradona play. Maradona makes £40,000 a game, all money which the spectators have freely given him. The 'fair' pattern has been upset. Liberty has upset the pattern.

Modern liberals at one extreme of the spectrum argue that property that is justly acquired should not be taken away for any 'social' reason. Absolute property rights accompany human rights. They see transfer payments made by government as questionable. Putting a free citizen on the dole is 'confiscating money from someone else'. 'People who say they have a right to state support are saying they have a right to your pocket book,' says Walter Williams. Income tax is theft because you work 'from January to the middle of May and don't get anything back for what you produce'.

> The most mischievous sentence in the Constitution of the United States was the sentence about providing for the 'general welfare'. What the Founding Fathers meant by providing for the 'general welfare' was not food stamps. They weren't talking about aid to dependent children. They meant that government should only engage in those programmes that benefit *all* Americans, not specific Americans but *all* Americans. National defence, that benefits all Americans. Having courts to adjudicate disputes, that benefits all Americans. Enforcing contracts, that benefits all Americans. The legitimate functions of government are those things

that benefit all Americans. But what we have now was insightfully described in H. L. Mencken's definition of an election. He said that an election was an 'advance auction on the sale of stolen property'. Politicians run on a promise: vote for me, and I'll use the power of my office to confiscate the property of one American citizen and give it to another American citizen to whom it doesn't belong.

Liberal economists also argue that there is no basis for assuming that voluntary charity and private insurance would provide less than governments today provide in transfer payments to the needy. Few wish to scrap the whole of the welfare state. Nevertheless, in Britain and America researchers like David Green are rediscovering the mechanisms that preceded the welfare state – municipal hospitals, local school boards, welfare charities – discovering what a rich array of 'giving' they provided. They note that inter-state 'giving' is voluntary and that the capitalist countries of the world contribute most, with the United States providing some 60 per cent of all international aid.

Nevertheless, the notion of a moral space at the centre of human life, where an individual has to decide what is good and what is not, implies a certain danger. A philosophy which says something is good just because it makes us better off has a hollow centre. Does the liberal follow rules? What will they be?

These are questions which Frederick Hayek has addressed late in his life, and which he explained to us in one of the first major interviews for our project. A 'rationalistic age', which has an answer to everything and thinks it can explain everything, has a problem with morality. It accepts only what it can explain. It may easily, therefore, dismiss 'traditional rules' of behaviour. He calls this 'the fatal conceit'; for suppose these traditional rules are codes of behaviour selected by evolution, necessary to the survival of the group. If we dismiss them as 'superstition' we take a risk. The search for new knowledge has a way of showing that these 'symbolic truths' are there for a reason. Incest and marriages between close relatives were taboo in primitive and ancient societies thousands of years before anyone understood the genetic weakness that results from the pairing of kin. Much conventional morality, under attack from rationalists for two centuries, turns out to be logical and efficient.

Hayek goes on to make some more distinctions. The laws of morality have nothing to do with laws passed by governments. Most laws passed by governments do not deserve the name. They are administrative orders, attempts to solve political or managerial problems. Moral laws or rules are not like government laws. They are inherited, selected by evolution, part of our human capital, complex, difficult to fathom, obscure in their origins, apparently irrational. But they work. That is why they have been passed down. They are available through the medium of the culture into which we are born. Like language, the laws of morality have been assembled over generations by our forebears. They are products of no single mind.

Traditional notions of morality do not generally appeal to intellectuals. They like things they can analyse or argue about. And they regard a traditional morality as a constraint, as if people who follow traditional rules are somehow not free. He argues that is wrong.

The novelist Ayn Rand used to call popular films and TV programmes 'bootleg romanticism', by which she meant that they carried profound meanings frowned on by the intellectual establishment. The academic critic of popular culture generally argues that popular culture (or mass culture, as he will probably prefer to call it) parades a 'rhetoric of individuality' which is false. We disagree. It carries subtle themes of freedom and morality.

Let us take the despised wrestling match, watched and loved everywhere, and a perfect image, for some, of bestiality.[11] In the wrestling match, a subtle and meaningful play is going on. The important bout is the match between the good man and the bad man. The rules of wrestling, like the laws of society, are not perfect. Nor are they perfectly applied. In fact, in a wrestling match, the detection rate for serious crime is low, for the referee is often looking away when the audience cries 'Foul!' The crucial moment of the crucial bout is that moment when the good man, under terrific provocation, enraged by a negligent referee and a totally villainous opponent, breaks the rules himself and revenges himself on the bad guy, who of course has been breaking rules all along. If the good man leaves this to the right moment, he will get the audience's support. Our hero may take the law into his own hands and play the vigilante. In other words, do not rely on man-made law. Pure social justice does not exist. You must look after yourself.

Popular notions of right and wrong are sometimes referred to, disparagingly, as the 'baggage' of popular drama. Often it is stronger than that. Here is the American critic Pauline Kael talking about the film *Dirty Harry*: 'In the action genre it's easier – and more fun – to treat crime in a medieval way, as evil, without specific causes or background. . . . fascist medievalism has a fairy-tale appeal.'[12] Research evidence shows that popular opinion on such subjects as capital punishment is rather complex. It is, however, likely to be 'moral', stressing retribution, rather than 'pragmatic', which is the position of those who are against capital punishment because they do not believe that deterrence works.

A social democrat calls a traditional morality 'fascist' because it does not look for causes or take time to forgive. The 'liberal' (not in our sense) critic always carries the hope that human nature, tended right, will one day bloom as in a garden. Seen from another eyeline, however, a personal morality is liberating. It enables me to make up my mind and act. It tells me what to do, without forcing me to refer upwards. It frees me from dependence on the say-so of another. The fact that it is 'traditional' should be a truism. It is obvious that no morality could be original with oneself. A traditional morality is what each generation inherits from the past, which it tests and tries and may improve. It has generations of knowledge and experience built in. Its survival shows that it worked. It is what all human beings inherit and need to inherit to survive.

Our soap operas are samplers, helping people to make up their minds and do the right thing. A pretty girl gets an offer to go off with a man who runs a modelling agency; is he on the level? Should I go to college and leave my boyfriend behind? Michele is pregnant; what is she going to do? You have to answer those questions, yourself – that's freedom. With luck you have a family and some attentive friends, and an attentive soap. Morality is protection. In liberal societies, morality is not authoritarian or 'fascist', but, increasingly, a matter of personal choice. The many religious channels on American cable TV offer a selection of moralities. Pat Robertson and Jerry Falwell are cultural entrepreneurs, supplying a moral need.

The political achievement which is valued most by ordinary people is stability. Stability lets them get on with their lives and accumulate personal possessions, improve their capital. An enormous amount of our popular culture has been preoccupied with questions of law and order. But every private eye is protecting the classical liberal values of freedom from force or fraud, protection of property and security of contract, and defending a framework of rights first described by John Locke.

A few people suggest other uses for the moral space that liberalism provides. One of them is Ayn Rand. As we have seen, she was a Russian émigré who wrote popular novels, like *The Fountainhead* (1943) and *Atlas Shrugged* (1957), which proved astonishingly popular. But she is loathed by most of the academic world. She attempted to reformulate, in her novels and essays, the natural rights of John Locke. Her philosophy is one of 'ethical egoism'. It proclaims the 'virtues of selfishness', vindicating the rights of individuals to exist and to act for their own primary good.

Ayn Rand's theory is an aristocratic theory of excellence reborn in the twentieth century. A person's life is a project, which he or she must strive to make outstanding. Our main role in life is the exercise of rational self-interest in the pursuit of this objective. Wealth is but a measure of success. If some are permitted to excel to the limits of their abilities others will be raised too. It is the same process that ensures that no athletic record ever stands for long. 'Selfishness', for Ayn Rand, means taking care of yourself, conserving your human capital, and investing it in your life's project. Selflessness is failure, for it squanders a once-and-only chance of excellence.

If the intelligentsia is unimpressed with Rand's philosophy, it will be even less impressed with Ed Snider. He owns the Philadelphia Flyers hockey team and looks a bit like Blake Carrington of *Dynasty*. He is the main financial support for the Ayn Rand Institute, and became a disciple after reading *Atlas Shrugged*, which, he says, cleared him up on something he had been bothered about. People used to ask him why he worked so hard, and he used to feel 'confused' and have to answer that it was 'just for the money', which he knew was not really right. '*Atlas Shrugged* told me that work is a man's life and money is only a measure.' Snider likes to illustrate his views by talking hockey. 'If we pretended all hockey players were the same, we wouldn't have a team, we wouldn't even have competitive sport. Some players are better and they should be allowed to excel. They bring the others up to their level. The good players help the ones that aren't so good and they all win the championship.'

Ayn Rand's moral philosophy is directly opposed to the evolutionary idea advanced by Frederick Hayek. With Ayn Rand you should make all your decisions by the light of your reason. With Hayek this would be a 'fatal conceit'. For him a moral code is the result of generations of trial and error. It contains more wisdom than any individual can obtain and we trifle with it at our peril.

These controversies run deep. There is a strain of anxiety among one group of New Enlightenment thinkers. In 1943 the economist Joseph Schumpeter wrote a book which argued that the very success of capitalism would produce an anti-capitalist class which would bring about its downfall.[13] One of his arguments was that the leisure which successful capitalism produced as a side-effect, increasingly taken for granted, would undermine respect for self-sacrifice, prudence, providence and the entrepreneurial virtues on which capitalism is based.

Others have since expressed similar fears. Some feel that the 'selfish' virtues that capitalism encourages must lead to a breakdown of the unitary state, of the debts and obligations and norms that are needed to maintain it. One group who feel this way are the neo-conservatives, represented in the USA by men like Irving Kristol and Daniel Bell, and in Britain by Roger Scruton.

Neo-conservatives are worried about the links between traditional morality and free-market economics. Kristol does not accept that a capitalist system produces the morality needed to sustain it. On the contrary, he thinks that the free market has a tendency to subvert traditions, having a turbulent effect upon culture and morality. That is why the neo-conservatives adopt an attitude that is not 'economic'. 'We are bourgeois,' says Kristol. 'It is bourgeois society that produces the kinds of people who make a free market work and who make capitalism acceptable. . . . The first job of a civilization is to produce a certain kind of person.'

> What we are looking for is an intellectual way of connecting the free market with an attitude towards life that is not economic but derived from religion or at least from traditional values. . . . A free market, in and of itself, doesn't tell you what kind of person to produce. A free market involves only the exercise of self-interest within a limited sphere, namely the economy. But you need an ethos that tells you how to raise your children, whether you should marry or stay married, whether you should be loyal to your friends or to your government. I don't like the contradiction between individualism and collectivism. In fact, most

Americans are both individualist and communal, rather than collectivist. We all belong to communities of some kind, religious, fraternal, professional. These play an important part in our lives.

The New Enlightenment cannot resolve the ultimate moral question. Its adherents are united in the view that socialism is *the* truly conservative philosophy of our day. Socialism is retrogressive. Yet socialism still lays claim to the moral high ground. It is good. It is about fairness and about sharing. It is about community, the warmth of solidarity, meeting the enemy together, helping out a friend. Frederick Hayek thinks that socialism is a kind of atavism, a longing for our hunting past. 'In a sense, we are all socialists,' he says. 'We are still governed by feelings that are based on what was necessary in the small group of people among whom each had to aim at fulfilling the needs of the persons he knew. . . . Our instincts still tell us to strive to serve the needs of known people. Our pleasure in life is derived from the consciousness that we follow a set of common purposes with people whom we know and who share our environment.'

Hayek thinks the desire for social justice is a call from this old instinct. 'Distribution according to merit', he says, 'would only be possible in the small groups from which we derive our intuitive instincts. Abandoning social justice was the price we paid for developing large societies.' So there is a socialist and a liberal in every psyche, memories of the hunting band, active and ambivalent, something biologists of the future will have to tell us more about.

We still feel that atavistic crowd pleasure, the collective thrill of a war or crisis. These instincts do not foster the peaceful reciprocal trading habits of a developed market, which started when tribes learned to leave spare goods on their boundaries and found upon their return that something useful had been left in exchange. With this, the impersonal graces of civilised life began.

Our search for rules of behaviour has pointed to large areas that are not well understood. We can now move on more confidently, to a canard of our times: the hatred directed at a wealth creator. Our thinkers concur in believing that each of us must be free to use our own knowledge for our own purposes. The web of society is woven from private choices.

4
Making It

One of the most impoverishing illusions in the world today is the bizarre concept that wealth creates poverty, that somehow some people are poor because others are rich. The idea itself perpetrates more poverty than almost any other concept in the canons of Marx.

George Gilder, in conversation

The suave defender of the corporate state begins his address as follows:

> In the old days, if you believed in personal liberty, then you also believed that a businessman was free to go out and make money by producing whatever goods and services he could sell. It is not like that any more. Today we have big, big corporations who form monopolies with ease. That is the reason why we have to control them. It is not individuals who create wealth these days. It is big companies, smoothly working machines, manned by thousands of people. The people who run these companies are not capitalists in the original sense of the word. They are 'managers'. Management is a skilled professional occupation. Big companies are no longer owned by buccaneer capitalists but by pension funds and savings institutions. New products emerge from well-organised research departments. In fact, it is rather like the modern state. Everything is big, organised, centralised and controllable. So there is no reason why the state cannot work with these big companies, work out targets for the nation, back winners when the nation needs to make big strategic changes in the direction of its industry, develop a new aero-engine or the fifth generation of computers. Stability, skilled people and a clear sense of direction is what our people need.

This chapter is heavily influenced by conversations with Akio Morita, Sir Peter Thompson, Israel Kirzner, George Heilmeier, Antonio Martino and, above all, George Gilder, whose work informs almost all of these pages.[1]

There was a time when our imaginary defender of statism would refer to France as the model country, and speak of the wisdom of France's 'indicative planning' system. Now that France has turned away from dirigiste central planning the example is more likely to be Japan. Japan Inc., he will tell us, is the true modern corporate state, where a few large protected companies work hand in glove with Japan's Ministry for International Trade and Industry (often known as MITI).

In the face of this progressive change, old-fashioned capitalism will disappear. Its seedy, unlovable characteristics will be retired to the golf club. What Edward Heath called 'the unacceptable face of capitalism' will be painted out. Some images attack the very future of free enterprise in a democracy, our corporatist explains. The sack of dollars shipped out of Grand Cayman in a Lear jet. The hard-faced boss and his ill-equipped, unsafe factory (it has been in the family for generations). The rogue financier, buying and selling companies, and building pyramids of paper.

Hold on, we say. We have come to talk about entrepreneurs. We do not know these people you mention. But we have to tell you first that a stable state is an illusion, born of a perpetual desire to find easy solutions to the problems of an economy. A stationary state means poverty, decline, disease and despair.

Entrepreneurs are the givers of the modern world. They are the altruists of the day. They create things that afford pleasure. They take leaps in the dark. The entrepreneur uses hunch, intuition and imagination. He floats on a sea of subjectivity called the market. The entrepreneur is motivated, like an artist, by the desire to create. He or she responds to the needs of others. It is in the hope of satisfying others' needs that an entrepreneur concentrates on producing value. A greedy person is a person who extracts comfort and security from others, perhaps petitioning a government to give it to him. The entrepreneur goes for challenge and creativity, the challenge of responding to the needs of others. Capitalism begins with saving and thrift, not with avarice.

New Enlightenment writers are discovering that entrepreneurs are the neural system of the market, transmitting and generating information. Entrepreneurship is about the division of knowledge. Entrepreneurs are *the* discovery procedure. Multiple risk-takers in the market make multiple guesses at what others want. The new economics regards the risk-taking, opportunity-perceiving function of entrepreneurship as the most creative and valuable social role.

But making mistakes is what entrepreneurs do most of the time. The market for goods moves rapidly. Entrepreneurs, like all participants in the market, speak the language of price, especially price expressed through futures or interest rates. This is why government intrusion into the signalling system makes it harder. Inflation clouds the cybernetic feedback. Markets are information-rich. Command economies can gain access to only a tiny proportion of this information.

Let us fly across time zones to Tokyo, the favourite exemplar of the successful corporate state where companies work hand in hand with a government planning agency. This notion is not completely untrue. During the post-war period MITI took control of licences for the import of foreign technology, the supervision of export funding, the strategic planning of basic industries. It helped the great pre-war trading companies or *zaibatsu* back on their feet again. As in Germany, industrial reconstruction was a top priority. Many people of talent and ability were seconded to it. In spite of all this, the image of MITI as the pilot of Japan's post-war economy is quite misleading. George Gilder, who has spent a lot of time trying to fathom Japan's industrial success, reckons he has talked to more electronics industry executives in Japan than any other American. He is scathing about the role assigned MITI:

> You can discuss the electronics industry with its leaders for hours without a single mention of MITI, which many Westerners think was crucial to achieving Japanese success. The

fact is that the Japanese have been successful in electronics virtually from the 1950s when Sony dominated the world market in transistor radios. The idea that planners targeted the developments of the fifties, the move into consumer goods in the sixties and the move into the production of memory chips in the seventies is totally mythological. Government spends less money on the electronics industry in Japan than the USA or Britain. If you go to any country and seek out what government does, you're going to be able to find ways that it has had an impact on electronics. Intellectuals like other intellectuals. MITI is an organization full of intellectuals that specializes in grandiose plans, projects, and white papers that discourse on the future of the world and the importance of the information era. Western intellectuals, who are sceptical of their governments, nod very solemnly when they hear these announcements and ascribe to these officials this very broad-based massive thirty-year miracle.

The rapid growth of the Japanese economy is, in Gilder's view, mainly correlated with the number of firms in the system.[2] Japan has far more small firms relative to its gross domestic product than Britain or the USA. It has seven times as many manufacturing firms with fewer than fifty employees as the USA. It has as many small businesses as the USA with half the population. Japan has twelve automobile companies compared to three in the USA, more calculator firms, more robotics companies. 'It's a pullulating arena of business competition. And that's why it has grown faster.'

In a country supposedly dominated by large conglomerates it is interesting to note that at various times during the last few decades there have been fifty-eight integrated steel firms, fifty motorcycle companies, and forty-two makers of hand-held calculators. Today, in the mid-1980s, there are sixty-five personal computer manufacturers, thirteen makers of facsimile machines and 250 producers of robots.

To what does Akio Morita, joint founder of Sony, ascribe

Japan's success? For a start, MITI has no involvement with Sony's present planning. 'They don't tell us what to do or interfere with our autonomy.' Does Sony discuss its plans with MITI? 'No,' said Morita sharply, 'that's a trade secret and they might tell other people.' He says MITI helped to build up the basic industries after the war.

Morita thinks it is much more important that the 'Japanese saves to secure his future. If the general public start to depend on the government, people will lose independence. I'm delighted that the Japanese people still have such a high savings rate. It shows that they want to secure the future for themselves.' Morita also refers to the numerous competitors that arrive in the wake of every new development. 'A hundred people now make Walkman-type machines. Our biggest competitors are Japanese companies.'

The other ingredients in the mix are social and political. 'Japan has some kind of consensus. Communication is good. We are a very homogeneous people.' But he is not talking about the kinds of 'formal tie-ups' between government and industry that he sees in some European countries. Since the government takes 50 per cent of Sony's net earnings in tax, Morita says that the government should feel like 'one of our shareholders. The government should help because they get the benefit.'

A recent World Bank study shows that countries, including Japan, with low or declining tax rates have increased their state income much faster than countries with high or rising tax rates.[3] How do they do it? They take it from greater growth.

Sony's business story does not tell of a smooth gradient of success ascended arm in arm with government. Masaru Ibuka and Morita wanted to make a domestic audiotape, having started doing contract electronics work for the government. MITI would issue no import licence for the base material for tape made by the 3M Company in America; so Sony tried to develop a new kind of tape out of paper. MITI then switched tracks, changed its mind and let in the base material. The new company was stuck with a good team of technicians and an invention that no one needed. Although their attempt at paper tape did not come to anything, the effort of trying to make it work paid off. To compensate for the fact that it broke so easily, they developed better circuitry, recording heads, and amplifiers for the tape recorder itself. That kind of advantage was to make Sony the leading supplier of high-technology equipment to the world's TV industry.

When Sony made tape recorders the conventional way, they found that there was no demand for the product, forcing Akio Morita to go out and create one. He persuaded courts to start making audio transcripts, teachers to get into audiovisual learning. The first 'pocketable' tape recorder was too big for a shirt pocket, so Sony actually made shirts with pockets large enough. They were creating their demand curve. Sony sold half a million of their first model and one and a half million of the second. It was while they were launching the Type 63 'pocketable' tape recorder that the company changed its name from Tokyo Tsushi-Kogyo Kabushiki Kaisha to Sony, derived from the word 'sonic'.

The attempt to pioneer a brand-new kind of tape left Sony with a human asset, a group of smart technicians with nothing to do. Ibuka went to America to look for a patent, and found Bell Laboratories working on the transistor. During 1953 and 1954 he fought with MITI to get permission to import the licence and exploit the technology. They were reluctant to give it to a young company, preferring, in their civil service way, to pass it on to a big trading company like Matsushita. They said they could see no use for this technology. Sony finally got permission, and made a portable radio. Before anyone knew that such a product was possible, Ibuka said to his workers: 'We are going to make radios – small enough so each individual will be able to carry them around for his own use, with power that will enable civilisation to reach even those areas that have no electric power yet.'

Sony were not the first to make a transistor radio. But the partners had an enormous desire to please customers. The Sony radios, marketed in America under the name Eagle, were the ones that worked. The Sony story makes a nonsense of the idea that entrepreneurs face given supply and demand curves for their products. There was no one out there saying 'I want a portable radio' when Sony went to market. Sony created markets. They were inventing the future.

Sony is now a famous multinational. Since the war the corporate planners have had a love–hate relationship with multinationals: hate because these giant companies are felt to have greater powers and more autonomy than politicians or nation states; love because an established multinational company is just the sort of company a social democrat would like to bring into the planning system. Socialism, it has been said, appeals to intellectuals because it emphasises the things they are good at: analysis, rationality, abstraction. The trouble is that many large companies which are making established products in a predictable market have reached the defensive phase of their lives. They are not likely to be innovators and they are likely to be losing employees.

Many of the companies that do succeed in these vital areas, creating new jobs and discovering new needs, are either small or behave in ways that have much in common with small companies. They have recreated the conditions under which entrepreneurs thrive. But recent research by the American Christopher Freeman does not support a 'small is beautiful' myth. The decisive factors are not small size or informality, but the presence of competition and an intense interest in the customer. Competition is the torque that drives innovation.

Talking to Akio Morita about Sony could not be less like talking to someone who thinks he knows a market or takes the future for granted. Morita thinks that the most important responsibility of the men at the top is to 'define the product'. Having the scientific and technical skills to make the product is only one story. Then comes the planning of production and marketing. Perhaps we should call it 'making a market'. 'Marketing is education,' says Morita, and illustrates it by explaining how he had to go out and create a market for tape recorders.

A successful new product is not an invention; it is the discovery of a need. Take Sony's famous Walkman. The new idea here was that people might buy a small portable tape player with no record mechanism, thereby reducing its size and making it suitable for a pocket, with the listener using a headset. 'A lot of people in our company didn't think the machine would sell,' says Morita. Now they are everywhere. Many other companies make them. There was certainly no visible demand schedule for a Walkman.

It is up to the people at the top to define the values. Morita says he likes to 'play tennis with young people, ski with young people and see what kind of interest they have. Ibuka is a great reader, with great curiosity, interested in toys.' Inside the company, discussion is continuous. 'You cannot say "Do this. Do this." We are always exchanging ideas.'

Texas Instruments is a firm run in the new way that emphasises innovation and inventiveness, a big firm aiming for small-firm characteristics. A successful firm in an innovative field must learn, according to George Heilmeier, senior vice-president, to 'motivate the best people'. It cannot afford class barriers and must be flexible to change. At Texas Instruments there are no executive perks, no chauffeurs, no limousines. The chief executives are called by their first names.

Texas keeps its innovative people by its willingness to risk research funds. 'We put a big premium on innovation.' They take many approaches to it. One of them is an 'idea programme'. The firm gives $25,000 towards the cost of the research and development of any project selected by a jury of the workers' peers. TI's 'Speak 'n' Spell' toy came out of this programme. At any one time there are about a hundred of these schemes running. After selection a team is put together to help refine and embellish the idea.

Ideas can come from many different sources at TI. Scientists, salesmen, marketing people. 'The important thing', as Heilmeier says, 'is to execute the idea.' The 4-megabit DRAM

(Dynamic Random Access Memory) was a major development of Very Large-Scale Integration chip technology. An idea came into the mind of a TI employee travelling to Tokyo. Instead of watching the movie he was thinking about the architecture of the chip. The conventional way of making chips used a planar structure. The minute microcircuits are spread in layers. He had the idea of designing trenches into the silicon wafer. He tried it out on his friends and they agreed it might work. TI put a research and development team round the innovator and they produced the first 4-megabit DRAM.

The reward for success is honour, money and peer-group recognition. But in a system made for innovation there has to be a freedom to fail. 'If you want to surface the best ideas, you can never make people look stupid. Don't keep scores. There are times when you must forget and start anew. If people feel like a failure, they'll never do anything.'

Britain had many good reasons for the far-reaching privatisation programme that began with the arrival of the 1979 Conservative government. Britain's nationalised industries were unpopular, and an industrial disaster, inefficient and expensive. Governments were finding it increasingly difficult to meet their investment and borrowing needs without exceeding the Public Sector Borrowing Requirement target, an important aspect of government economic management. The British were seeing in action the public monopoly's tendency to grow and grow without any concomitant public gain. The Conservatives had talked in their election campaign about getting big government off people's backs. But it was a rather pleasant surprise to realise how much the sale prices could add to their revenues.

In fact the British startled themselves by their world leadership in the new art of privatisation or the sale of state assets. The first privatisation exercise was almost inadvertent. British Petroleum was largely owned by the government, but it had the legal form of a limited-liability company and its shares were traded on the exchanges. Its directors decided to make a share issue, which was not taken up by the British Treasury. This diluted the state's holdings, and, to the satisfaction of both politicians and directors, BP became free of its connections with the Public Sector Borrowing Requirement. In 1979 the new Tory government decided to sell some shares and harvested hundreds of millions of pounds it had not realised it owned. It dawned on Treasury ministers that not all state corporations need be liabilities. Many coherent trading units could be sold.

British Aerospace went first, then Cable & Wireless, the old imperial telecommunications giant, then Amersham, a specialist research and development firm. The London financial markets enjoyed the new experience, and London started to attract the interest of other governments, who thought they too might have hidden assets available to be brought to the market.

The largest privatisation exercise since Henry VIII sold the monasteries was the sale of British Telecom. The auctioning of this giant corporation inspired governments in every continent. Although the sale of the nationalised gas utility will be a larger exercise than BT, the sensation of fresh air gusting into the murky world of state monopolies excited more than brokers or bankers. Two million individuals bought shares. It broke psychological barriers. The monopoly was hardly relaxed but the complacency of the old public corporation had gone. The British Treasury reckon they have now given seminars to sixty-eight other governments whose interest had been triggered by the BT sale. The most remarkable converts were the Japanese, who decided to sell off their state railway and telecommunications agencies. Government discovered, as the public-choice theorists had predicted, that the very notion of competition is enough to stir up sluggish public monopolies.

In Britain asset sales are running at £5000 million a year, almost 5 per cent of the yield from income tax. Britain has led in the new techniques of privatisation. But the Turks and Italians have also discovered how far and fast they could push back the frontiers of the state. Turkey sold the Bosphorus Bridge. The state airline THY is now being offered on the market, beating British Airways off the runway. All of Italy's state holding companies, legacies of fascism, are being offered to buyers or to employees.

New thinking is melting old assumptions. Markets are seen as liberalising forces. Even communist China has been seized by the enthusiasm for markets. Britain may have surrendered Hong Kong but the free-market colonial enclave is converting the rest of China. Property rights to land and housing stocks are being re-established after fifty years of obliteration. Collective farms and factories are turning to profit-sharing, and to profit-seeking.

With few nationalised industries the United States has not shared in the asset-sales bull market of the 1980s, but it has been in the vanguard of deregulation and liberalisation. It is said that Eastern Airlines managers read the essays of Frederick Hayek on pricing before deciding to allow ticket prices to be negotiable. Municipal bodies have found they can save money and enhance the morale of their employees by auctioning off duties such as refuse collection, laundering and catering. Ambulances, museums, parks, cemeteries, fire departments and nearly every other municipal service has been opened to competitive tendering. We are seeing the tangible result of thought, the downstream effect of work started by the Mont Pelerin Society.

A variation on privatisation by stock-market flotation is to hand the assets of the public body over to the workers. The sale of the National Freight Corporation's assets was a model of the new economics. The new owners became sensitive to prices. And within a few years they were much richer. Today NFC employees, pensioners and their immediate families own 83 per cent of the issued shares. The remaining 17 per cent is held by the banks who provided finance for the purchase of the company. NFC workers shares are now worth twenty-seven times their original value. Britons know NFC as Pickfords, the storage and removals people.

Over the four years since denationalisation, the company's turnover has increased from £438 million to £700 million. Its trading profits have increased from £14.6 million to £40 million. It has bought Merchants Home Delivery Service in California, along with transport companies in Hong Kong, Singapore and New Zealand.

The irony of the success of the National Freight Corporation's sale of assets to its employees was that it would have been floated on the stock exchange if it had not been for previous losses and the underfunding of its pension funds. Sir Peter Thompson became chief executive in 1977. He holds that position today, and was able to tell us about the difference between then and now. 'The old company was governed by the constraints of the public purse, by how much the state could afford to put in. We were never able to invest more than £55 million when we were state-owned. Last year we invested £100 million. And we could never offer a wage larger than the government norm.'

A more fundamental change occurred when the firm moved out of state ownership. When Herbert Morrison set up the nationalised industries the hope was that people would be cared for and that the industries would be caring. But these huge concerns were not 'people-focused'. Sir Peter showed us his latest business plan, and compared it with what had been written in the days when NFC was a public company. In those days it had said nothing about 'people'. 'Today it's all about motivating people.'

He concludes that the state is too abstract to inspire people's enthusiasm. Now things are 'closer to home'. The firm can say: 'We want you to be loyal to this enterprise, and if it goes well you get a piece of the action. If you can improve its efficiency, you can also improve your profits. You can't feel that way about UK Ltd.' Looking back, Sir Peter identifies the problem of the centralised monopoly: 'If you set up a centralised monopoly, it becomes an argument between powerful trade unions and a powerful monopolistic management.' NFC now avoids centralism. It conducts negotiations at a local level. On the other hand, its annual general meetings attract 2000 and more shareholders, debating the future of the company. 'It's a cross between a political rally and a genuine business meeting,' says Sir Peter. People find the video shot at the annual general meeting profoundly moving. Thompson finds it strange that the British left does not support what he is doing.

The three companies we have looked at are people-oriented. They accept that their most precious resource is people. Their companies have been designed to stimulate and respond to the needs of people. They also control their operations more by shared values than by formal rules. They evoke highly motivated efforts from their staff by providing an opportunity for employees to act innovatively. They keep separate operations small enough to allow for initiative. They provide employees with various forms of 'positive reinforcement', ranging from sales success rallies to the provision of amenities for personal work. They all design products in close proximity to their customers.

The most famous and influential book on business management in recent years is called *In Search of Excellence* (1982) by Thomas Peters and Robert Waterman.[4] It stresses the importance of a 'value system', and the numerous ways in which employees are encouraged to think innovatively and work in small ad-hoc, shifting groups: 'product champions' are appointed (making one person solely responsible for the success of a new innovation), 'skunk sessions' are set up (sending teams away to come up with something), a time limit is set for 'performance shoot-outs' (putting two teams on the same project and inviting them to compete), etc. Among the images from this book that stick in the mind are Thomas Watson, founder of IBM, sweeping aside piles of complaints that had been carefully sorted into categories and declaiming, 'There's just one problem here. Some of us aren't paying enough attention to our customers.'[5] Bill Hewlett of Hewlett-Packard, taking a bolt cutter to a locked equipment closet and leaving a note saying, 'Don't ever lock this door again.

Thanks, Bill.'[6] Caterpillar Tractors offering its customers throughout the world free parts if the tractors are not delivered within forty-eight hours.[7] These and similar tales create motivating myths, which guide the employees of an excellent company more surely than formal priorities.

In this world the firm begins to seem to have a different function from firms of old. The old firm was a hierarchy run by a boss. A new firm is a machine for increasing the exchange value of individuals' skills and abilities, providing a framework within which employees can realise their best creative potential. The firms are people-oriented. The skilled move in and out. What matters for the rest of us is that the entry of new entrepreneurial small firms into the market is assisted in every way.

The idea of encouraging entrepreneurs informs numerous corners of policy. Freeports and enterprise zones, ideas scarcely heard of a few years ago, now account for an expanding proportion of international trade. These freeports are the equivalent of the constellation of little institutes and think tanks spreading the capitalist or libertarian message around the world. Freeports are miniature enclaves where entrepreneurs are licensed to be free of conventional taxes and duties, planning constraints and bureaucratic impediments. They are the opposite of discretionary regional aid or the state development agency. The turnover and range of goods and services traded in the freeports is growing more rapidly than any other element in the world trading system.

Britain and Japan are two island nations. One is an economic success. The other is now an economic failure. How did the Japanese let their entrepreneurs flourish?[8]

The principal instrument which produced these contrasting outcomes is tax policy. Successive Japanese governments have enabled individuals to accumulate large amounts of accessible savings, available to launch thousands of companies, some of which have failed and some of which are now leaders in their field. While Japan has achieved an unprecedented rate of growth, Britain has promoted 'the stealthy and unannounced euthanasia of the entrepreneur'.[9]

The hero of Japan's revival is Tanzan Ishibashi, Japan's Ludwig Erhard. He was the first to see the critical link between fiscal policy and an entrepreneurial business strategy that would rebuild Japan's economy. Japan's economic ascent began when he took control of MITI in December 1954. He insisted that the key to economic growth was not government subsidies or guarantees, but whopping tax cuts.

He focused his tax cuts on personal incomes and personal savings. It took a while for the good idea to be recognised. Ishibashi was Minister of Finance in the first post-war cabinet, from which he was fired for opposing an American-inspired austerity programme. 'The only way to solve the problem is to promote production,' he had said. Japan was still stagnant in 1950 when there were tax rates of 85 per cent on moderate incomes, a tax burden of 24.1 per cent of GNP, and a persistently high inflation rate. Around this time the American economist Edwin O. Reischauer declared that 'The economic situation in Japan may be fundamentally so unsound that no policies, no matter how wise, can save her from slow economic starvation.' The economy was again in recession when Ishibashi took office in 1954. Ishibashi did not lower tax rates for established and profitable corporations. His first cuts came in 1955 when interest rate tax was abolished, dividend tax was cut by a third, from 11 to 7 per cent, and most personal taxes were cut by 10 per cent. Corporate profit tax was cut by a tiny fraction from 42 to 40 per cent. The results were inspiring. Within a year, tax revenues actually rose by 15 per cent and savings did too. Between 1950 and 1974 Japan was to cut rates annually by an average of 11 per cent a year. Yet at the end of the process tax revenues, the Japanese government's income from taxation, were four times greater than the nation's GDP had been in 1950.

In the year Ishibashi died, 1957, he cut personal taxes by 30 per cent across the board. New companies like Sony benefited. They launched their pocket radio in 1955, well timed to take advantage of the growing disposable income Ishibashi had generated. The other side of his policy was the creation of incentives to save. Not only did he abolish tax on savings interest and reduce tax on dividends, he also tripled the level of tax-exempt savings with the national banks and doubled the deduction for life insurance. The success of his strategy was such that for twenty-five years government revenues grew faster in Japan than in any other nation while government spending as a percentage of the total economy remained one of the lowest. Japan was able to increase its government revenues during the 1970s by 33 per cent more than Sweden and 44 per cent more than Britain, all financed out of growth, reducing the tax burdens on individuals.

By exempting interest from tax Japan was able to get itself one of the lowest interest rates in the Western world. This factor was far more important than special industry protection in fostering the global expansion of companies like Hitachi, Matsushita, Honda and Sony. The high Japanese savings rate and resulting low interest charges have permitted literally millions of Japanese businesses of all kinds to expand their investments over the last thirty years.

British policy, by contrast, has been the direct opposite of Japan's. Since the First World War, Britain has pursued a policy of progressive taxation and penalising personal saving. The evidence that tax revenues rise during periods of tax-cutting has been ignored. The failure of progressive taxation to provide government with the revenues it needs has resulted in a poverty trap. A system once meant to redistribute money from the rich now actually takes taxes from people in poverty. Britain's marginal tax rates are now among the highest in the world. Even after Mrs Thatcher's tax cuts the top rates remain at 60 per cent on earned income.

The British tax system creates a culture of perks. Low-paid managers, facing high marginal tax rates and unable to build up savings are compensated with company cars and generous business allowances. The effect of high tax rates is invariably to move people from taxable to untaxed activities, from investment at home to foreign currency ploys abroad, from offices and factories to golf courses and grouse moors (a high tax on work income makes leisure more attractive), from new products to old houses, keeping the capital gains, from small businesses into the arms of large well-established companies with pension schemes for government departments. 'Most of all, high taxes redistribute the British themselves' to Grand Cayman, Nassau, Monaco. A diaspora of the country's most creative individuals has taken place. Some of Silicon Valley's most celebrated entrepreneurs are British: Alan Osborne and John Ellenby in personal computers; Wilf Corrigan and John Carey in semi-conductors.'[10] It is significant that 90 per cent of all high-technology companies in Silicon Valley began with the savings and mortgages of individuals.

So a high-tax country like Britain becomes a country of conspicuous display, a country where the rich waste their money. The 'unacceptable face of capitalism' is not that of a rogue businessman or greedy capitalist: it is that of a tax avoider with nothing useful to do with his money, living in a climate hostile to enterprise.

Tax policies that have learned the Ishibashi lesson are called 'supply-side' policies because they liberate the energies of people, stimulate activity, generate innovation and increase the supply of goods. The supply side is liberated by tax cuts. The supply side of an economy may be diverted, but not suppressed.

On paper Italy looks like one of the poorest countries in Europe. The Italian economy is very heavily regulated. The government appears to control the economy through a plethora of hugely inefficient state investment holding corporations. Vast amounts of taxpayers' money are sunk without trace into these organisations, in order to pander to the demands of politicians and vested interests. The bureaucracy is so swollen and inept that it is mocked as *lacci e lacioli* (shackles and snares). According to national statistics the average Italian is a lot worse off than the average Briton.

Yet, if a British traveller visits Italy today, he will see that statistics lie. The Italians are better off than we are. Other, non-standard indicators tell us more of the truth. Italians import more champagne and whisky than anyone else in Europe. They have more second homes per capita. They take more holidays than anyone else. Italy exports millions of gloves to other countries, but there is no official record of glove manufacturers.

The Italian spirit has a fortunate mistrust of bureaucracy. It is estimated that 10 per cent of Italian trade now occurs in the submerged or 'black' economy, the *economia sommersa*. In 1979 Italy's statistics office acknowledged that it was reasonable to raise GNP estimates by 10 per cent and to cut unemployment figures by one million to account for the black economy.[11] Some estimates put the size of the *economia sommersa* at 20 per cent of GNP and the underground workforce at around three million. Others put it at six million.

The Italian civil service is one source from which the *economia sommersa* gets its workers. Italian civil servants officially work from 8 a.m. until 2 p.m. every weekday. Although the pay is not marvellous they have complete job security and receive substantial retirement pensions, health insurance and fringe benefits. In their afternoons they are free to work in whatever 'underground' organisation they please. Every few months there is a newspaper article about how one of the ministries is trying a new method ensuring that its officials arrive on time and leave at the official hour. Italian ministries have been defined as buildings where those arriving at work a bit late meet those on the stairs who are leaving a bit early.

Sometimes the *economia sommersa* can give a tax holiday to a developing industry. Around Florence, in a district called Prato, is an industry employing 160,000 people making high-quality woollen textiles. Today most of them are officially recorded. In the 1950s you would not have found a factory registered anywhere. The industry survived and prospered by staying in family-sized firms, holding production in units of less than a dozen employees. That meant they could avoid registering for social security contributions. The area was successful because in its early days the avoidance of tax and social security kept prices down. But the quality of their designs and products made these manufacturers among the best in Europe. Today the area has gone legal. Although most artisans still have looms in sheds at the back of their homes, Prato has switched, on the strength of its success, to more capital-intensive methods of production. It has become successful, so it can afford to use less labour-intensive methods than before. The Prato grew to its present position from the small undeclared home workshops of the 1950s and 1960s.

The same thing is unlikely to happen in Orvieto, a small cathedral town about 120 kilometres north of Rome. Its narrow, medieval streets contain numerous small workshops or *botteghe*, producing pottery, wooden furniture, wrought iron and lace. Most of them are family concerns. Most of them operate in the *economia sommersa*. Some have tried to expand. Some have even taken on apprentices. But social security payments, health insurance payments and volumes of form-filling drive them back to the family unit. One artisan told us that social security payments amount to 90 per cent of an employee's salary. These high labour costs keep operations small.

One company is slightly larger than the others. Paolo Fusari makes plates, jugs and ashtrays for restaurants and hotel chains all over Italy. He effectively employs ten people. However, enquiry reveals that his three potters are really a separate company. Every jug must be invoiced and recorded, before it is passed across to Signora Fusari. Why does Fusari not employ them? After all, they were once his apprentices. His wealthy accountant (another drain on the entrepreneur's resources) explains that there is no tax for the employer to pay on an apprentice's salary.

Professor Antonio Martino is an authority on the Italian black economy. He estimates that the average Italian is about 30 per cent better off than he would appear to be on paper.[12] He puts the underground workforce at 15 per cent of the total. Martino argues that the black economy is of general benefit, though he agrees that everyone would be better off if neither the regulations nor the black economy existed. It has the disadvantage that it criminalises society. When the threat of opening up bank accounts to scrutiny was first advanced the Bank of Parliament was crowded with MPs closing their accounts, as anxious as any other bank customers.

In spite of its disadvantages, the *economia sommersa* has done well for Italians. They arranged for their own supply-side tax cuts by ignoring taxes. It has made all Italians better off. Citizen deregulation made a little economic miracle.

As tax rates have climbed and regulations have multiplied in European countries, more and more people are pushed outside the law. In Britain, too, nearly everyone is involved in the black economy at one time or another, paying for the odd item or service in cash or in kind. The obverse of the black economy is an excess of display. The Rolls Royces in London's streets are an expression of the 'British disease', a sign of idle money or a tax-free perk, a waste of enterprise like Fusari's accountant.

Human beings are ignorant but well able to learn. The entrepreneur is teacher and explorer both, transmitting new information to prospective customers about better uses of their time or money. This is the exact reverse of the position adopted by Marxists. Marx regarded entrepreneurs as expropriating or exploiting the labour of others. This Victorian view percolated wide and far into popular sentiment, accounting for the doubtful social status of people in 'trade' rather than 'public service' or the professions. The capitalist could be as kindly an individual as could be wished. He was still, by definition, an exploiter of his workers.

The new regard for enterprising individuals contradicts more than Marxism. It repudiates the entire British tradition. Adam Smith had a dim opinion of businessmen: for it was 'in spite of their natural selfishness and rapacity' and in spite of the fact that the 'sole end they proposed' was 'the gratification of their own vain and insatiable desires' that they were 'led by an invisible hand' to advance the interests of society. Adam Smith was one of the greatest friends the market idea has ever had but he fathered a deep contempt for 'projectors and undertakers'. Yet entrepreneurship is the oxygen that gives life to the rest of the economy. It is so powerful that it fizzes away in command economies. Bribery, corruption and the black economy arise from attempts to obliterate the entrepreneur.

The entrepreneur may not be a business executive. He is as likely to be an artist or scientist, an artisan or a craftsman, an engineer or a retailer, driven by a desire to create and explore where others have not yet ventured. The failure to see the importance of the entrepreneur has been a crucial one for the twentieth century. Keynes could commend them only for their 'animal spirits'.

If Adam Smith, Karl Marx and John Maynard Keynes all got it wrong, how did this come about? The answer requires a diversion into the textbooks. In the British economic tradition the national economy consists of a large but fixed set of product categories. Each has its 'demand schedule', which estimates the differing amounts that would be bought by customers at different hypothetical prices. (It is obvious that you want to buy more strawberries when they are in season. The price goes down.) Each product also has its 'supply schedule'. This represents the differing amounts that would be manufactured at various prices. (If strawberries kept their winter prices all summer a lot of farmers would switch over to strawberry fields.) The supply and demand schedules can be represented on the famous XY graph that appears in the economics textbooks. If the vertical axis represents the amount that would be produced and the horizontal axis the various prices, the demand line will fall and the supply line will rise as you read from left to right. Where the two lines cross is the equilibrium point. That says what will actually be produced and what price it will fetch.

These graphs were invented by Alfred Marshall to clarify

the ideas of Adam Smith. Adam Smith thought that value and price were largely the result of how much labour had been expended. The British tradition therefore treats profit as a kind of reward or wage for the job of supervising industry, making a process as efficient as possible, supplying the demand for a product at a slightly lower price and winning a larger share of the market. The rewards for the entrepreneur, however, have no clear connection with the work done. This British tradition sees the national economy like a great chemical plant. There are unloading bays for raw material, endless pipeworks for circulating process material, combustion chambers for the various processes, and outlet points for a great variety of intermediate and finished goods. The quantities of the inputs and outputs are known. There is nothing to invent, nothing to create.

Marx inherited the Smith tradition, which made it easy for him to argue that entrepreneurial activity was in a strict sense a theft from the workers because their labour was the only source of value. Marx says that the sale price of a product derives from the costs of the inputs (that is the raw material inputs and the fixed assets such as machinery, which are gradually 'consumed' as they wear out). Then there is the value added by the employees. The owner or capitalist pays for the inputs. If the sales returns exceed these costs, that represents the value added by employees. If this is not returned to them, it has been stolen. Every capitalist is an exploiter.

The classic refutation of Marx's theory of capitalism was published by an Austrian economist called Eugen von Böhm-Bawerk.[13] He published his book in 1896, between spells as Austrian Finance Minister. Marx's *Capital* had appeared two years earlier.

In the first place, Böhm-Bawerk argues, it is wrong to think of value as congealed labour. Everyone must know that he can spend hours of labour on something quite useless and unsaleable. Value, he argues, derives not from the past but from the future, not from the history of production but from the expectation of consumption. What someone will pay depends entirely on the satisfaction he expects a product to yield him. This is wholly subjective, often irrational, but the value of the goods derives from the enjoyment they will later give. The value of a steel rolling mill, for instance, comes from the millions of car journeys and convenient appliances it will produce.

To clarify the position the Austrian school even made a distinction between the capitalist and the entrepreneur. The entrepreneur, even when working with borrowed money, makes a profit or loss by setting on production. The capitalist just lends his money out at the standard rate of interest. In truth, the entrepreneur lives in ignorance. The supply–demand graphs of English economics are a bad description of reality. Entrepreneurship consists not in making decisions in the light of your knowledge of supply and demand schedules, but in trying to discover what the schedules are. Both demand and supply schedules for any good are not stable; they are in a state of unpredictable motion. The schedules shift, as a consequence of human creativity. Someone thinks of a new method of production. A new product is created. In the 1960s, there was no demand or supply schedule for the word-processor I am using to write this book.

From these shifting and imperfectly known schedules come the profits of the entrepreneur, who gets some range of inputs to produce something different from before, as did Mr Mars, who saw a pile of offal and dreamed of dogfood. But an entrepreneur's profits are temporary. While they last, they may be enormous. The bigger they are the more an entrepreneur has added to our stock of relevant knowledge. Profit and loss do not come from discovering an equilibrium. They come from disequilibrium, deviations from the norm.

Today, the leading interpreter of the Austrian school is Israel Kirzner. For him, the discovery of this 'pure profit' is the whole purpose of the entrepreneur. The entrepreneur 'notices the opportunity for pure gain. . . . The future of capitalism depends on what cannot be foretold. It depends on the creativity of the human mind. That is why no one can predict what capitalism will produce. If the human spirit is left free, it will create what no one has hitherto imagined to be possible.'

To Austrian economists, therefore, an economy is a network of relationships between people. The British tradition sees economic life in terms of aggregates, a range of options defined by supply and demand schedules. British economics therefore maintains that the 'market' defines the opportunities of entrepreneurs: 'entrepreneurs merely scout the marketplace and mediate among existing demands, making transactions that maximize their own self-interest as expressed in power or profits.'[14] The Austrians say entrepreneurs make a market. Like artists, they bring new things into the world.

The British intelligentsia, however, educated in a mixture of Marx and Adam Smith, ended up with a limiting view of the entrepreneurial role. Many socialist traditions looked towards a growing mastery over the natural world and towards the increasing mobility of our species within it. The Italian communist thinker Gramsci says unequivocally that the object of socialism is to 'transform' nature.[15] Marx greatly admired the productive power of the nineteenth-century ironmasters, and wanted it incorporated into a socialist society.

The British view is static. It crystallised at a time when Britain was the most prosperous country in the world. No one, apparently, had any doubts about our future productive potential. Indeed, by the end of the nineteenth century our productive potential was seen, mainly, as a scarring, disfiguring reality brought by economic growth. British thinking was comfortably redistributive and the middle-class intelligentsia turned against productive economic activity. Its creativity, and the culture that accompanied it, was channelled not into increasing our mastery over the universe, but into a decorative local culture, wistfully retrospective, complacent. This genteel and static tradition formed Britain's intelligentsia and passed into the twentieth century.

It is echoed by Maynard Keynes in a passage in *The General Theory*, little noticed, in which he makes the most extraordinary prediction. He looks forward to a period, some fifteen years ahead, when the problem of poverty will have been solved. The passage deserves to be quoted: Keynes starts by assuming that 'steps have been taken' to ensure that the 'rate of interest is consistent' with 'full employment'. He then assumes that the state also ensures that the 'growth of capital equipment shall be such as to approach saturation-point at a rate which does not put a disproportionate burden on the standard of life of the next generation.'

> On such assumptions I should guess that a properly run community equipped with modern technical resources, of which the population is not increasing rapidly, ought to be able to bring down the marginal efficiency of capital in equilibrium approximately to zero in one generation; so that we should attain the conditions of a quasi-stationary community where change and progress would result only from changes in technique, taste, population and institutions.

In other words Keynes believed that in one generation it might be possible to satisfy human needs and aspirations to the extent that entrepreneurship was no longer needed. This means that the opportunity to invest at interest disappears, or, as he puts it, the 'marginal efficiency of capital' goes to zero. Note that Keynes identifies the investor as a rentier capitalist – not what we would call an entrepreneur. He goes on:

> If I am right in supposing it to be comparatively easy to make capital-goods so abundant that the marginal efficiency of capital is zero, this may be the most sensible way of gradually getting rid of many of the objectionable features of capitalism. . . . A man would still be free to accumulate his earned income with a view to spending it at a later date. But his accumulation would not grow. He would simply be in the position of Pope's father, who, when he retired from business, carried a chest of guineas with him to his villa at Twickenham and met his household expenses from it as required.[16]

Lacking a theory of wealth creation the British intelligentsia is today unequipped to handle the problem of poverty. Individual creativity is applauded in the artistic sphere, condemned in the economic sphere. Socialism looks for big solutions, twitting the British multinational GEC for not investing enough. Conservatives are only just beginning to lose their dirigiste habit of thought, which imagines innovation as happening in a research department of the technostructure. This tradition cannot distinguish entrepreneurship from individual research.

Why do big established companies seldom launch major innovations? Concentration occurs in an industry not, as per socialist theory, when the most powerful company gobbles up the less strong, but when the future becomes known. Then and only then do those supply and demand schedules stabilise. At this point the pace of innovation slackens and the emphasis is put on economies of scale and marginal gains of efficiency. The research departments of large companies have always been primarily engaged on these two projects. The funds that establish them are the proceeds of a stable and predictable business environment. Even the big research agencies, though they may present themselves as hothouses of invention, are in fact funded by companies working in established sectors, and looking for marginal efficiency gains.

Crucial inventions happen at moments of great uncertainty when a collective approach would limit the possibilities. A collective approach cannot provide the divergent and complementary shots at a target that are needed. They *are* needed when a major new discovery or invention offers potential benefits, but its use and application are not clear. That is a period of upheaval and uncertainty. Concentration may follow as the new shape of things emerges. But in this unstable first phase, in the phase where new products are being born, there is no risk equation that can reasonably draw savers' money or public funds.

If no equation can be made between risk and gain, the innovator might be making an economically irrational decision. That is why many entrepreneurs are lone individuals. The entrepreneur is not the margin-watching, canny, calculating, vulgar person defined in the British tradition. Innovation evades calculation. It may depend on personal accident, on a small inheritance, on a screaming need, on obscure discontent, on a second mortgage, on an uprooted career, on who knows what? As George Gilder has it, 'Entrepreneurs are more likely to find inspiration in a pink slip than in a promotion.'[17] Entrepreneurship is a crisis.

George Gilder has done more than anyone to map the contours of the entrepreneurial personality in our time. He himself credits A. David Silver, leading student of the psychology of entrepreneurs. Silver discovered, in an extensive survey of major American successes, that most were driven by conscious feelings of deprivation and guilt stemming from broken families and connections.[18] Many had lost their fathers through death or divorce. Some, like Vietnam veteran Fred Smith, founder of Federal Express, underwent the trauma of combat and came back to win another kind of war at home. 'In the modern age, however, the paramount source of entrepreneurial disruption and guilt is the turbulent politics of a tyrannous and war-torn world. In nearly every nation, many of the most notable entrepreneurs are immigrants.'[19]

Gilder writes about the incredible successes achieved by Cuban immigrants in Florida, building up a string of large-scale businesses and occasioning this quotation from Chamber of Commerce leader Lester Friedman: 'The best thing that's happened in Florida since air-conditioning was when Fidel Castro read Karl Marx.' The immigrant is a man who is uncertain of his link with the future. George Gilder: 'It is the link of particular men to particular children that orients the society towards the future, that gives man a very incarnate sense of their future, and that drives the kinds of long-term commitments that are indispensable to achievement and to entrepreneurship.'

In his diffident, unassertive Japanese way, Suneo Takatori

says he wants to 'produce something completely different, something not made elsewhere'. He was inspired by the robot in Fritz Lang's film *Metropolis*. Four years ago, at the age of twenty-three, he gave up his studies in classical Japanese and Egyptology, took the £4500 his parents had given him to put himself through college, and invested it in a company. His parents were mortified. Takatori and his collaborators work night and day, writing software on assemblies bought cheap at Akihabara, Tokyo's micro-chip street market. His company is worth £750,000 and growing. He says: 'I want to produce something that lasts. We are limited only by the compass of our imagination.' The Ibuka–Morita spirit is going strong.

Entrepreneurship, as George Gilder reminds us, is hard.

> Most entrepreneurs I know get up at five in the morning. Important activities absorb those who pursue them. The crucial efforts are always the marginal efforts, the efforts to push beyond existing constraints. It's hard to keep the world going. Business creativity entails mobilising more resources than writing a book or painting a picture, and people who teach classes or write books resent the idea that business may command large sums of money. To take this away merely forces them to apply to some board of experts in order to expand their operations, and as soon as that happens an economy collapses.

Enterprise is unstoppable. The entrepreneur is on the leading edge of an instinct we all share. It emerges wherever it can and goes off on its poverty-slaying mission. In Italy citizens deregulate unilaterally and improve their lives. In Japan, sensible tax decisions make way for its beneficent work. In America, a tradition of individual freedom preserves much of the wealth-creating potential of the human spirit. In command economies and in old-fashioned welfare states poverty deepens.

5
A Constitution for Liberty

There is practically no single factor which has contributed more to the prosperity of the West than the relative certainty of the law which has prevailed there.

Frederick Hayek

We are at the frontier. The pioneers fan out into an empty land. The plots have been marked. Each pioneer can claim one, and establish a legal right to ownership. Pretty soon conflicts develop, as they will. A line on the map of a new territory may not mark a boundary clearly. The pioneer needs some agency to resolve differences and to protect him from the depredations of his neighbours. This may lead to a protection agency, perhaps an armed group led by a strong man. There is a danger that the strong man will form a private army, seizing the holdings of others until all the new settlements fall under his sway. He becomes a king or a feudal lord or the leader of an authoritarian regime. Such rough solutions do not lead us to the modern liberal state.

Try it another way. The new protection agency behaves in a more 'commercial' manner, deciding to build up its client list. It does not pay to have clients in open conflict since it can only represent one of them. Though the agency has an armoury, settling conflicts by armed force is risky and expensive. Better to settle claims between clients by peaceful means. So the agency develops negotiation and arbitration skills. It still has the use of force at its disposal, but it prefers peaceful settlements. Soon it will be refusing membership to families who use force unilaterally or do not follow its code of conduct. Gradually the advantages of a large and stable agency become clear. The 'market' settles on a few major agencies.

We have received great help in the writing of this chapter from Richard Epstein, Oliver Letwin, Norman Barry, James Buchanan, Kurt Furgler, Claude Massy and A. E. Dick Howard.[1]

The agencies apply their own codes of conduct to their own clients. Sometimes they have to resolve claims between their own clients and those of other agencies. It makes sense for agencies to reconcile their justice systems. As the agencies co-operate they develop other services. With the use of force in their repertoires, they provide protection not just from the aggressive intentions of individuals, but from organised bands of outsiders, attracted by the wealth of this ordered, peaceful and co-operative community.[2]

We are on the way to a liberal state. Some would call it a 'minimal' state, or a 'night-watchman' state. It is inspired by the notion that the peaceful enjoyment of our own property and the free pursuit of our own ends, in communities in which others are likewise free, comprise the highest political good. The scenario above shows how this state grows logically from a negative right: the right of individuals to use their own property for their own purposes without interference from others. It is not, of course, the way actual states have developed.

Not all New Enlightenment thinkers agree that we want a 'minimal' state. They all agree, however, on the importance of the tradition of the 'limited' state, whose job it is to safeguard the rights of individuals. This tradition says that a state is no more than the individuals who compose it. It opposes any system of thought that treats the state as more than the sum of its individual parts. This tradition, to which John Locke contributed and of which the American Constitution is a product, begins in England.

At Runnymede in 1215 the Magna Carta was signed. In the Magna Carta various arrangements and ideas are formalised which must have been part of the unwritten constitutional order of Anglo-Saxon politics. One idea is that a citizen who participates in government is also protected from government. Another idea is the notion of 'common law', which supports the civil rights of ordinary people as opposed to 'court law', which is law enacted by the king. 'Common' law defines the rights of the individual against the authority of the state. Common law is also a residue of past experience. In the words of political science professor Gottfried Dietze, it is 'accumulated by jurists over ages [and is] superior to the natural reason of the living'. 'Common law' is the vehicle of individual property rights. In the Magna Carta property rights and other civic rights were part of the same package. Gottfried Dietze finds that of the charter's sixty-three chapters or sections, thirty-eight deal with property rights; only twenty-three protect other rights.[3]

In a half-century of English civil war in the middle of the seventeenth century, the boundaries of power between king and 'commons' were fought out. That process ended with the Glorious Revolution of 1688. John Locke was its political philosopher. In the work of Locke we find a modern description of the rights of a free individual. Individuals, he says, should have the 'freedom to order their actions and dispose of their possessions as they think fit . . . without asking leave or dependency upon the will of another man'.[4]

John Locke was the son of a country lawyer from a small village in the English county of Somerset. He was educated at Westminster School and at Christ Church, Oxford, where he later became a don.

It is in his *Second Treatise on Government* that Locke developed the theory of political sovereignty that has become the basis of liberal political thought. He begins by imagining a 'state of nature' in which there is no 'common judge with authority' or, in other words, no established system of law and order. In such a system, what would the 'law of reason' prompt each human to require? Locke concludes that we would want peace and quiet and the freedom to get on with our own lives. As he puts it, the law of reason 'willeth the peace and preservation of all mankind'.[5] When someone in the 'state of nature' violates this law of reason, vigilante action is justified. 'Every man may bring such evil on anyone who hath transgressed that law, as may make him repent the doing of it, and thereby deter him (and others) from doing the like mischief.'[6] Except in that one circumstance no one may 'take away or impair the life, or what tends to the preservation of the life, the liberty, health, limb, or goods of another'.[7]

The problem with private justice is that people are often bad judges in their own case. A private system will be full of 'inconveniences'. It is in order to remedy these 'inconveniences' that a civil magistrate is set up. But that magistrate (king, parliament or Supreme Court judge) has no more power than what is given for the purpose of enforcing the 'law of reason'. If this magistrate fails to enforce the law, or departs from it, or exploits his position, he puts himself 'in a state of war' with the people. They are 'absolved from any further obedience' and free to 'resume their original liberty'.[8] They may choose to set up some other legislative system to provide for their peace and security. All political authority comes from the people. Government is a contract. If it fails to keep its side of the bargain, it loses the right to govern, and may be overthrown. This is the argument so succinctly put by Thomas Jefferson in the Declaration of Independence a century later.

In John Locke's words, 'goods' are one of the things, along with all that 'tends to the preservation of life . . . [and] liberty', that must not be taken away by another. Indeed Locke asserts that the 'reason why men enter into society is the preservation of their property'. When they 'mix their labour' with property taken from the common stock, they make it their own. This is the basis of our entitlement to what we own. We are free to exchange what we own with others for anything they themselves hold justly.

This framework has stood the test of time. Although philosophers have tried hard to dig down to a stronger foundation for natural rights, the attempt has on the whole been a failure, although the American philosopher Robert Nozick offers the following argument for the recognition of natural rights. A person, he points out, has only one life. So there is no good that one separate person can gain from being sacrificed, without his consent, for the good of another. A state, which claims an individual's allegiance (as other individuals do not), must at all times be scrupulously *neutral* between its citizens. It should never be party to actions which use one person as a means to another person's end.

John Locke wrote, when he was a don at Christ Church, his two treatises on government, which concluded that governments were no longer legitimate if they were not safeguarding the liberties of the people. They were probably written in 1681 to justify the rebellion of the Duke of Monmouth. Locke was a known activist, and spies in Oxford watched his movements prior to the rebellion. He left the country after Monmouth's failure. The two treatises were finally published in 1690, after the Protestant revolt that brought William and Mary to the throne, and it became known as the Glorious Revolution of 1688. His words still held sway one hundred years later, when the American people decided that the rule of George III was no longer legitimate, for just the reason Locke outlined. The Declaration of Independence in 1776 and the American Constitution of 1787 are two of the finest liberal documents ever written. In the century since Locke wrote, the liberal tradition had gained breadth and strength from other sources.

The American Constitution of 1787 was an attempt to answer this question: how do you run a government while limiting that government in the interests of individual liberty? The constitution came in two stages. The first stage set up a system of government with checks and balances and a separation of powers. In this separation nobody is allowed to exercise the power of any other. Many legislative rights are reserved to state legislatures. 'Judicial review' may strike down acts of Congress which are beyond the legislative powers of that branch. No bill may become law until the President assents to what has been passed. These were the safeguards designed to protect the liberties of individuals and the autonomy of the separate states.

During the period since 1776, the states had conducted their affairs like separate countries, developing separate legal systems, even passing tariff laws against each other. The Anti-Federalists, as they were called, did not think the protections in the constitution were adequate, and it had to be ratified by nine of the thirteen states before it could be put into effect. So the Federalists agreed to add a bill of rights at the first Congress. James Madison undertook that it would be introduced. The bill was put to the country and very quickly ratified. To compose a bill of rights the framers drew on the so-called English Bill of Rights that came out of the Glorious Revolution.

The principles of limited government which received political expression in John Locke were, by 1776, generally shared by thinking people throughout the Western world. Government is a social compact: there are natural rights which individuals enjoy antecedent to government; when a compact is agreed these rights must be maintained against whatever state is set up. The US Constitution is, therefore, a Lockean document and a paradigm social compact. Only those powers spelled out in the compact are to be retained by government. The powers not conferred are retained by individual people.

The idea of independence did not just come from intellectual tradition. It was rooted in the historical experience of the American people. From the first settlements early in the seventeenth century through to the Stamp Act of 1755, America had experienced what amounted to self-government. British Parliaments had paid little attention. But after the wars that were fought in Europe and America in the eighteenth century, Parliament was looking for ways to raise revenue. One of them included making Americans pay a tax stamp on selected goods from Britain. There was an outcry after the passage of this act. The slogan 'no taxation without representation' became the battle-cry.

During the long period of benign neglect, the colonists had created forms of self-government. Temperamentally, they were individualists. Few habits of caste and class carried over from the Old World: no nobility, no trappings of the old order. America was the frontier of civilisation. On the frontier men and women fend for themselves, without authority figures to tell them what to do. Leaders like Jefferson and Madison leaned on the theoretical underpinnings of the Enlightenment to give constitutional voice to this experience.

A new, late strand in their thinking came from Scotland. The Scottish Enlightenment of the late eighteenth century was a very distinctive element of the Enlightenment and it had a profound influence on the American Constitution. During the latter part of that century that remarkable group, based in Edinburgh in Scotland – economists, political theorists and what we would now call 'sociologists' – all empirical by bent, developed a science of government which merged historical experience and the close observation of human nature. They were clear-minded about the weaknesses of human beings. They believed that people try to do the right things, but often fail. As James Madison put it, 'if men were angels, Government would not be necessary.' A government must guide the course of human affairs, but because it is run by human beings, its power must be held back. Human beings are fallible; human institutions are liable to abuse. We should only surrender our sovereignty where necessary.

James Madison, most influential of the framers of the Constitution at Philadelphia in 1787 and introducer of the Bill of Rights, had studied at Princeton under John Witherspoon. Witherspoon was a Presbyterian cleric who had recently come to Princeton University from Edinburgh, bringing with him the ideas of the Scottish group. Chief among those ideas was the argument, developed by Adam Smith, that though individuals will selfishly pursue their own interest, they are led 'as by an invisible hand' to serve the public good. The American Constitution is coloured by ideas that came from Edinburgh.

As for Locke, his work was in every educated American's library. It was certainly in Jefferson's. In the Declaration of Independence Jefferson reformulated Locke's 'life, liberty, and property' as 'life, liberty, and the pursuit of happiness'. Academics have had fun imagining why Thomas Jefferson changed these words. Did he exclude 'property' because he was talking about 'inalienable rights' and property *is alienable*, in the sense that – unlike life or liberty – everyone has the right to dispose of it when they choose. Hannah Arendt thinks that the pursuit of happiness to Jefferson meant the joy of involvement in public affairs. At the time of the Revolution Americans participated fully in public affairs, having established the tradition of 'town meetings' that the Frenchman Alexis de Tocqueville so much admired when he visited the country in 1846. We will never know. But because the Declaration of Independence denounces numerous British violations of property rights we can presume that 'happiness' includes enjoying one's own property. The Bill of Rights of 1791 later spelled out that neither 'life, liberty or property' was to be taken without 'due process of law'.

There was ambivalence among the framers about democracy. They wanted ultimate political power to be vested in the people, but they also wanted barriers of protection against the absolute sovereignty of a majority. The Declaration of 1776 is certainly a democratic document. It states that all government power derives from the consent of the governed. In a continental thinker like Jean Jacques Rousseau the democratic ideal included notions of the general will, of popular sovereignty, of unlimited rights writ large in the will of the people. (It was Rousseau who said the people should be 'forced to be free'.) But the American Constitution took precautions over the potential tyranny of a majority, and the harm it might do to the rights of ordinary citizens. The powers of temporary or transient majorities must be checked. Scope for what the founding fathers would have called 'faction' was contained.

When Jefferson died he asked for three things to be put on his tombstone. There is no allusion to the fact that he was President or Secretary of State. He reminds us first that he was the author of the Declaration of Independence, second that he was the founder of the University of Virginia, third that he was author of the Virginia Statute of Religious Freedom. The three achievements were what he regarded as the lynchpins of a free society: political independence, education in the rights and responsibilities of free citizens, and protection from those who would tell us what to do or think. In 1777 Jefferson wrote a Bill for the General Diffusion of Knowledge which would have created a kind of public school system. The bill failed of enactment. But he was able to found the State University of Virginia at public expense. He also designed the original university buildings, and there gave his ideas a physical representation. The neo-classical architecture of the University of Virginia is an invitation to students to observe the precepts of reason and to follow republican virtues.

The US Constitution (1787) and the Bill of Rights (1791) have stature as liberal documents because of the many different ways in which the individual was protected from the power of the state. The 1787 Constitution firmly entrenched a system of private property secured against the arbitrary use of force by government. The theory was defensive. It provided a space from which you could exclude all others. It permitted private individuals a sphere of autonomy and self-governance. The scope of public activity was controlled by indirection, by splintering the authority of government. It would be difficult, for instance, for the state to act with united force against individuals engaged in acts of commerce. First, because the separation of powers between the executive, the legislature and the courts provided a series of hurdles for legislation to pass. Second, because some activities, like intra-state commerce, remained within the discretion of the states. State power, in turn, could never be absolute because citizens were free to move from one state to another, thus providing a sanction against unpopular law. Freedom of contract, without which property rights cannot be implemented, was written into the 1787 document, thus defining the economic right of a free individual. The Contract Clause at Section 10 of the constitution declared that no state could pass a law 'impairing the obligations of contracts'. This was to become one of the most litigated clauses in the constitution.

Between 1787 and 1791 the deliberations of the framers moved on. They developed the notion that procedural obstacles were not enough to prevent a government from becoming a usurper of individual rights. So the protection of these rights was documented. Many were controversial at the time. Thus were established, as rights, the freedom of speech and of the press (Amendment 1) and the prevention of the taking of private property by government 'except for public use, with payment of just compensation' (Amendment 5). The framers had constructed multiple barriers against the 'power that tyrants can wield'.

How has this great constitution fared? Richard Epstein is James Parker Hall Professor of Law at the University of Chicago.[9] He is a follower of the public-choice school and has developed a series of legal arguments concerning the interpretation of the constitution. His answer to the above question is 'Better than most', in a world where constitutions have not been known for durability. However, Epstein thinks that much of the original constitutional promise has not been kept. The structure of checks and balances has worked quite well, and the mechanical provisions of the constitution have proved durable. It is difficult to argue over what 'two years' means when it says that is how long a congressman should serve, or to misconstrue the stipulations for the terms of office of the President and the Senate. In other areas there has been slippage. The rise of the great administrative agency at the time of the New Deal had the effect of combining the executive and the legislative branch in the hands of single bureaus, increasing the size and power of the state, and circumventing the checks and balances written into the constitution. The powers of the federal government under the so-called Commerce Clause have been strong. The Commerce Clause at Section 8 of the constitution permits Congress to regulate commerce 'among the several states', and the powers which central government has taken under this clause over, say, labour relations and welfare have been extensive. Other individual rights, by contrast, have been well protected. The Supreme Court has taken the doctrine of free speech seriously and has given a capacious protection to all forms of political discourse. If there have been periods when rights were overborne, as they were in the 1950s by the campaign of Senator Joseph McCarthy against 'communists' in government office, they have been restored.

In some fundamental respects, though, basic tenets of the original constitution have been reinterpreted. Contract rights began to suffer attrition during the nineteenth century on a nice point of law. The constitution prevents any interference with contracts, but perhaps the state can prohibit a certain kind of contract before it is formed? Perhaps government can place a prospective ban on certain kinds of transaction? By the closest of margins the Supreme Court decided that, although the state is required by the constitution not to impair the 'obligations of contract', there was, in the constitution, no general protection of the ability to enter into a contract. That left the state free to pass laws curtailing economic rights. Richard Epstein cites the *Lochner* case (1905) in New York as a watershed. New York State passed an ordinance limiting to ten the number of hours which bakers could work in a day. The bakers who pressed for the ordinance were unionised. They ran two shifts: one baked the bread the evening before delivery; the second took the bread to the market the following morning. The employees of the small independent bakers, however, baked the bread, and then slept on the job before making their deliveries. Mr Lochner, a small baker, sued on the grounds that the law violated his right to make a contract with his employees. He won, but the language of the decision was too weak to withstand subsequent challenges. Subsequently such laws became commonplace.

After the First World War there emerged what became known as the 'rational basis test' for interpreting the 'takings clause' in Amendment 5 of the constitution, which permitted private property to be taken for public use. The 'rational basis test' has meant that if a reason could be found for limiting the rights of property and the rights of contract, then the state was free to act. Prospective contracts could be stopped and uses of property could be curtailed. The main form of legal protection given to the individual property then became one by which no single individual or group could be selected out in a specific law. Although this is no trivial protection, it is not adequate to prevent something, anticipated in the constitution, which was called 'faction' by the late-eighteenth-century framers. Epstein explains:

> The simplest illustration is a situation in which 51 per cent of the people vote to confiscate the property of 49 per cent of the people. That could be done by general regulation. If the response is that it is not going to be tolerated, then one has to ask: What happens if 80 per cent of the population votes to confiscate the property of 20 per cent? It could go the other way. Powerful interests are very concentrated. It may be that through an adroit political lobby, 20 per cent of the population can confiscate the wealth of 80 per cent. The modern theory of political science treats individuals as self-interested actors, who will try to gain more than their fair share of wealth through the legislative arena if they can. This is a modern formulation of the ancient worry that concerned people at the time of the Founding Fathers. They talked about 'factions', meaning small groups of partisan individuals who turn the legislative process to their own ends. Faction works unless there is some kind of check.[10]

The Founding Fathers were alert to the fact that human beings are self-interested and imperfect. The 'rational basis test' is a weaker basis for the protection of economic rights than the constitution intended to impose.

The trouble was, in Epstein's view, that by the 1930s the American legal system had completely lost confidence in the equity of contracts. Even where contracts were not 'tainted by fraud and duress', they began to be seen as a system of oppression in which the stronger dominated the weaker. This went along with a loss of faith in the competitive economy to determine reasonable outcomes. A lack of 'fairness' of outcomes was seen as an inherent fault of the capitalist system, a fault that could be rectified by government. The role of government became one of redressing the balance.

Epstein is among those who regard this as an intellectual error of massive consequence.

> By the 1930s the dominant conception of contracts was this: contracts were an instrument of oppression in which the strong party took systematic economic advantage of the weak. The function of the government was to redress the balance by saying that certain kinds of contract could not be entered into at all. The key question for the modern political economist is: is this true? In my view, as long as there is no coercion involved in the formation of a contract, workers will enter in only if they are going to be better off with the contract than they would have been under some other circumstance. Why would they enter into arrangements that were going to lead to their personal ruin? The greatest protection for workers is a wide array of opportunities to work in as many different callings as possible. Regulation of the market place restricts entry. The simple model of contract, as an exchange to the mutual benefit of both parties, was lost sight of by the Supreme Court when they adopted a model of systematic exploitation. However, a belief in rational self-interest and the theory of limited government is incompatible with the idea that government must act to protect individuals who are incompetent to protect themselves. The intellectual revolution of the 1970s and 1980s rejects the idea that competitive markets are an instrument of social domination.

If a person is a self-interested and self-motivated individual, he will sign a contract only if it makes him better off than before. The individual and the community benefit by maximising the number of opportunities. That is achieved by a mobile labour market and freedom of contract. The insistence that an employer hires workers from one union or that he has to pay a minimum wage keeps poor people out of the labour market, limits jobs and creates monopolistic firms. This is how the liberal argument runs. Epstein believes it was embodied in the constitution.

Other modifications of constitutional limitations have come to serve the cause of contract interference. In particular, the 'police power' (government's duty to maintain law and order) has been extended, with the Supreme Court's backing, into zoning regulations, rent control and public health, on the grounds that this was necessary to protect social order.

Richard Epstein argues that, since the economic rights provided for in the constitution have been comprehensively abandoned, many economic restrictions could be questioned on the grounds that they are outside the jurisdiction of the lawmaker and so are infringements of constitutional rights. Will such arguments be upheld in coming years as the sense of the original wisdom of property rights returns to our political systems? Will the 'rational basis test' be viewed in new ways as the social costs of interfering with contracts becomes better understood? Will a restriction that tells an employer that he must deal with a union be thrown out as an unjustified 'taking' of private property when judges accept that it diminishes opportunity in the labour market? Will the Interstate Commerce Commission face a reassertion of states' rights and find its jurisdiction limited? Will courts recognise the violation of property rights (not to mention the harmful consequences) of minimum-wage legislation? (In 1950, the unemployment rates of young whites and young blacks were almost equal; today young blacks are deeply disadvantaged against their white peers in the labour market.)

To Epstein, it is a 'tragedy of modern times' that the interpretation of the constitution has:

> assumed that property is an artificial notion that is entitled to no respect. . . . The theory of autonomy recognises correlative rights of other individuals. You have to find a separate Me and Thee to make a theory of autonomy work. The only way you can do this is to have a system of property which says that certain things are mine and certain things

are yours. Property is not a system of greed. It's a social conception that gives people rights. It is associated with a general system of rules, which reconciles conflicting individuals with inconsistent desires, so that each of them, within the limits of scarce resources, can live lives consistent with those desires and not trample on the parallel rights of others.

Richard Epstein and others like him can take their views about fundamental rights back to the American Constitution. That cannot be done in Britain.

Britain does have a constitution. A constitution does not have to be written. People in Britain know when a law is a law and they know the respective roles of Parliament and the Prime Minister. The development of Britain's constitution, however, is strange and irregular. It grew historically out of a series of efforts to contain the arbitrary power of kings. The House of Commons became the bastion of defence against kingly power. Slowly this power has grown until it is greater than the king's power once was. The powers of the House of Commons are almost absolute. It is difficult to define what, if anything, limits that power. The unchecked power of the Commons is the primary fact of our unwritten constitution.

In Britain, we have no fundamental rights. Parliament could, theoretically, pass a law deporting all black people from the country, or requiring the police to arrest a Jew on sight, or sending anyone who obstructs a civil servant to gaol. We feel these actions would be un-British, but there is nothing in our constitution that describes them as illegitimate. This worry is not as ridiculous as it might appear. Times change. Today the state finds it legitimate to interfere with the running of a person's house in spite of the adage that an Englishman's home is his castle. It gives a statutory right of entry to many intruders; it tells a home-owner how to arrange the windows when planning a house; it tells a landlord how much he can charge in rent; it tells him whether or not he can get rid of a person who is living in his house. These restrictions would have been regarded as tyrannous in the eighteenth century. Today they are accepted.

At one time trade unions were regarded as illegal combinations. They were rescued from this unfair position; but then they were made exempt from pursuit under civil law. They were enabled to prevent people from working by the pre-entry closed shop. They were shielded from damages. Nor can anyone argue that these privileges are unconstitutional. In America one could challenge them. In Britain one can mount no common law defence against an act of Parliament.

This has left the British without anything that could be described as negative rights or liberties. This lack of fundamental and inviolable liberties goes almost unrecognised. British citizens have only such liberties as happen not to have been curtailed by Parliament. In the confused language of our time we do have 'positive rights', such as a right to welfare payments like child benefit or supplementary benefit, or a right to council housing. But if these are removed by Parliament or, worse, if negative rights or liberties are curtailed, there is no way an individual can complain, except, latterly, to the Court of Human Rights in Strasbourg. There is one written quasi-constitutional document, the Treaty of Rome, to which Britain is a signatory. This document renders some European Community legislation superior to that of Parliament. But there is no question that Parliament could take Britain out of the Common Market. In America, the Civil War determined that no such option was open to the separate states.

A positive right, entitling someone to a house or a free meal, imposes a duty on others without specifying who is to provide it. The state, therefore, takes on the job. The terminology of 'rights' silences discussion of the relative costs and benefits of such action. It deters rational examination of the effects of these transfers on the rest of the economy.

Although British governments have had members who take rights seriously, they seem ashamed to talk a language of rights, preferring to use the language of positive advantage or moral benefit. The liberty of the individual and the protection of negative rights are, largely, a closed subject in British political life, illustrating how deeply the language of positive rights and a mindset of socialism has permeated political brains.

Under this regime of parliamentary supremacy nothing protects the liberty of individuals from the tyranny of a majority, which could if it chose exploit a minority. The British system is therefore made for 'faction', well exposed to pressure for political decisions from powerful lobbies, the articulate or the noisy. Politicians are free to enhance their power. The few who worry about such matters are hesitant about the possibility of a British bill of rights which would enshrine personal liberties in an inalienable way. How could we constrain the power of Parliament not to alter it? Could a second elected chamber be given the power to veto legislation from the Commons? Could there, at the least, be a modest further use of institutions already established within the system, such as Select Committees, to review new legislation?

In the 1940s and 1950s the Supreme Court of the United States began to expand some of the guarantees embodied in the Bill of Rights. By the 1970s the Court had declared a zone, as it were, of privacy and autonomy round each person. A woman's right to have an abortion, say, or a couple's right to use any contraceptive method of their choice, were areas of individual discretion in which the state should have no part.

Western democracies have, over the last hundred years, seen a rise in civil rights, accompanied by a decline in economic rights. One of the arguments of this book is that civil rights are threatened by economic decline, and economic decline follows the decline of economic rights. A second argument is that 'positive rights' are a corruption of the notion of rights. They pre-empt discussion of transfers that may be inefficient and divisive. Many of these are an unjustified burden on the lives of others even when this burden is spread through general taxation.

The rights contained in British common law were gradually eroded as government took care of health and general welfare on a piecemeal basis. Then the 1906 Liberal government passed the historic Trades Union Act which set aside the common law of tort in cases involving a union dispute. This offered a model for the setting aside of common law rights in favour of powerful or influential groups. It opened the way to the emergence of a modern politics of accommodation in which parties win office by appealing to a coalition of interest groups with whom they compete for electoral favour by offering tax reliefs or some exemption from general rules. Appealing to the anonymous general interest is an obscure and unrewarding project by comparison.

In Britain the dictation of policy by outside groups is systematised in the Labour Party, where the trade union movement is a major influence on policy. The Conservative Party, too, has favoured constituencies, such as farmers. Both parties support the interests of home-owners, who benefit from a range of tax reliefs on mortgage payments which have no economic justification. In the process of interest-group affiliation, the implicit restraints of a homogeneous political society are loosened. The conventional rules limiting the powers of Parliament have been beset by interests and ideologies with no common conception of the system.

The lack of constitutional or common law limits means that a party with even a small majority faces no restraint on the passage of any programme it wishes. Without any separation of powers a winning party is sure, short of a backbench revolt, to secure the passage of its legislative programme. This is elective dictatorship.

It is a situation in which the law can constantly change, as one transient majority replaces another. It is not a situation which our political leaders will easily surrender, for they stand to win absolute power with tiny parliamentary majorities and with less than half the popular vote. To this massive widening of discretionary power, the liberal replies: human beings are fallible, power corrupts, and monopoly power will impoverish the community.

In an arena of such opportunity as the British Parliament, politicians become entrepreneurs, taking immense risks with their lives. The reward is not profit or even high wages, but an office of state. Parliamentarians widen their discretionary power. The Commons turns its upper chamber into a harmless replica of itself. The system spawns quasi-autonomous non-governmental organisations ('quangos'). The roots of local political initiative die when the solution to a new problem is always to take control at the centre. Alternating majorities put policies into reverse. The ship of state yaws. Out in the economy, nothing moves. The spontaneous order of political life is broken.

Not every nation is getting it wrong. In the gloaming of the twentieth century some nations stand out not only as commercially prosperous but as living within liberal ideals. The United States gave a liberal constitution to Japan. The Pacific rim of Asia has generated small states that have inadvertently found themselves with the human conditions of success. Hong Kong is a little pimple of entrepôt capitalism on the great backside of Chinese socialism. Its existence was a curiosity. The young naval officer who selected it as a trading post was reprimanded for choosing such a resourceless, useless, obscure spot. But given the light touch of British colonial power and the entrepreneurial zeal of the Cantonese, Hong Kong has become a stunning example of how, if states limit their roles to the enforcement of property rights, their citizens can flourish. These unusual states are repeated throughout history. The Netherlands were once the bits of boggy land the German princelings did not want. Yet the Dutch grew into a mercantile power, the greatest in the world in the seventeenth century.

The basis of prosperity is not a chance endowment of mineral resources or good land. Perhaps most anomalous of all the small-state experiences of success is Switzerland. The world thinks of the Swiss as a naturally prosperous and profoundly bourgeois nation. Yet it occupies the most disadvantageous terrain in Europe. Its geography is economically dreadful – a series of small valleys in between mountains that block all traffic. It includes racial or language groups that are elsewhere incompatible. For most of the last two thousand years Switzerland was regarded as the poorest, meanest part of Europe, but by a series of accidents and chances, the Swiss adopted a number of constitutional conventions that achieved a miraculous conversion of their nation.

The Swiss Constitution ensures the liberty of the individual and of minorities, includes formal and specific commitments to free trade and provides for a high degree of popular local initiative. The first line in the first article of the constitution states that the cantons or states are sovereign. The constitution guarantees basic human rights. It precludes the tyranny of the majority and allows for constitutional change by referenda. It provides extensive scope for public legislative initiative and protects the owners of property. It has an executive that is representative, emasculated and virtually anonymous. By 1980 the constitution had 123 articles. Law and justice to the Swiss are not what any temporary legislative majority happens to approve. They are set in abstract rules.

The Swiss jealously guard their property rights: Article 22 of the constitution specifically says that 'the right of ownership is guaranteed.' Provisions are made for the taking of property 'for reasons of public interest', providing that 'fair compensation shall be paid'. Some applications of this provision, such as expropriation for the compulsory storage of grain in times of shortage, are included in the constitution and have to be agreed by referendum. The right to secure ownership is protected further by the Federal Law on Expropriation which ensures that it can only occur as a matter of last resort. There is no equivalent of the 'rational basis' test.

Freedom of trade and industry are guaranteed in Article 39 of the constitution. The result is very low tariffs and no import quotas for manufactured goods. But the Swiss do impose import quotas on foodstuffs, to protect their farmers.

The Swiss have not had to yield to autarchic pressures of the

EEC. Even foreigners' property rights are protected. There is a law limiting the size of the federal establishment, and the budget has to be funded. Federal tax revenues amount to less than half the amount raised by the cantons and the 3020 communes into which they are divided. Direct federal income taxes affect only the rich. (Individuals with incomes over £40,000 pay federal tax at the rate of 5 per cent.) The federal government is not sovereign. Sovereignty lies with the cantons and with the people. The political culture is based on intimacy and propinquity rather than party. The checks and balances are so great that neither party nor faction can gain dominance. One characteristic of the success of Swiss political culture is the fact that no one outside Switzerland can name Swiss politicians. The Swiss seldom know their names either.

Switzerland is the most prosperous country in the world. Banking and financial services are only part of the Swiss commercial success, nor is tourism any more important than in other parts of Europe. Switzerland has a manufacturing and commercial sector kept alert by free trade. When its watch industry was threatened by the arrival of the Asian and American digital technologies in the 1970s the Swiss did not protect their precision engineers. They kept the trade doors open. The Swatch, a plastic fashion watch, was their answer to the digital invasion.

Switzerland was left as a loose confederation after the final defeat of Napoleon. Its unity was threatened by deep internal divisions, both religious and political. In 1846 a league of Roman Catholic cantons was formed, called the Sonderbund, with the object of separation. The Diet, which represented the other cantons, met at Berne and dissolved the Sonderbund. By swift military action it was able to end the hostilities. The resulting constitution of 1848, which borrowed heavily from the United States, provided a form of confederation acceptable to the various religious and language groups. Liberal in inspiration, it provided a parliamentary democracy in which people were able to elect two chambers and vote on all constitutional change.

The executive consists of a seven-member federal council, elected from the federal assembly. This ensures that it is composed of representatives of several parties, not just one. The powers of this executive body are more dilute than those of any other government. The presidential term is one year, and each member of the council becomes president by rotation. He is not the head of state; the federal council as a whole performs that function. The population have a right to referenda, which they describe as the right 'to say no when Berne says yes'. In other words, they can reject legislation proposed by the National Assembly in Berne. They demand referenda quite frequently. There are, on average, about ten a year. The right to referenda produces conservative decisions. The right to referenda may lead to conservative decisions. In Switzerland women did not get the vote until 1971.

Kurt Furgler was President of the Swiss Confederation in 1985. He arranged the first Gorbachev–Reagan summit. Then he went back to being a regular member of the council again. Was it an anticlimax? we asked. 'It made no difference,' he replied. 'We are co-responsible.' Claude Massy is the Liberal MP for Vaud. He owns and operates, as so many Swiss do, his own small estate, a vineyard of three hectares. Massy, like all MPs, is a part-timer who gets no salary for his political work. Playing cards with his friends in the cafe in the village, he is bemused when self-important French deputies visit him in their grey Renault 25s.

The Swiss cantons have a great deal of autonomy. At the time of the 1848 constitution, because of language and religious differences they were even more desirous of keeping their independence than the American states had been. The cantons retain control on all aspects of justice, police, social security and education that are not specifically granted to the federal government in the constitution, and any change must have been voted in by a majority of the cantons and the citizens. They have their own constitutions, directly elected parliaments and executive councils. Every canton has direct votes or mini-referenda on major local issues and their sovereignty is limited by their constituent communes. In some of the mountain cantons popular democracy takes place in a very direct way. In what is known as a *Landsgemeinde* the electorate meet annually in a town square to ratify and vote on major issues affecting the canton. At Glarus they have been holding such gatherings since 1387. The electorate is 22,000. About 10,000 turn up every year.

While we watched, the incoming president of the cantonal government was sworn in in the presence of the voters. The appointment of local judges was ratified. The voters proposed a new judge, but he declined. The main debate of the day was over the proposed widening of a mountain road. A commission set up by Parliament estimated that it would cost the canton SWfr 40 million (£15 million). The proposal was supported in the Glarus Parliament by 39 votes to 1. During the *Landsgemeinde* many people came to the tribune to speak for or against the motion. Speakers showed a card to demonstrate their membership of the commune. When it came to the vote, the people rejected the proposal. In spite of Parliament's recommendation and impassioned speeches in its favour by elected representatives, the road was turned down.

Switzerland, though, does not get a high turnout at elections. In the 1979 election only 48 per cent of the electorate voted. It has been down to 35 per cent. A sign of indifference? No. Elective dictatorship turns voting into a major life decision. High turnouts mean anxious electors. But the more control you have over your life and the more reduced are the powers of government, the less interest you take in a national election. Swiss elections do not usually change the party composition of the federal council, which in fact has not shifted since 1950. With the fundamentals of life and liberty set in the constitutions, the electors make a managerial choice at election time. The Swiss know that a widened sphere of discretion for the politician means a dented sphere of freedom for the individual. The Swiss lead stable, prosperous and free lives. The chance for clever people to conduct experiments with humanity has been denied. Remember Thomas Jefferson

He had other things to tell us on his gravestone than that he was once the President of the United States. Will the main achievement of the New Enlightenment be to take the illiberal heroics out of politics and give people back constitutions that set a limit on the politician's scope? The spontaneous order of Switzerland shows that it works.

6
Private Worlds

Clever men and women will always be interested in ideas.
That is what makes clever men and women so dangerous.

Paul Johnson, in conversation

Two intellectuals have dominated the way people think, talk and behave in this century: Karl Marx and Sigmund Freud. Marx legitimised grievances about the way some get rich and others stay poor. He told the poor that their poverty was caused by the structure of society. He told them that they, the majority, were exploited. Never mind, argued Marx, who starts things, who invents things, who takes risks. The source of value is labour and the fruits of this labour are yours.

Freud told us that everything we do or think is conditioned. We are moved by strange, unexpressed desires, repressed emotions, stirrings of events deep in our childhoods. This theory links up with Marx's idea that we are creatures of our socio-economic circumstances. Freud's thinking undermines personal responsibility.

Between them, these two savants inspired the growth of modern tyranny, what Paul Johnson calls the 'despotic utopia'.[1] The despotic utopia combines the idea that people can be improved or changed, using this new 'knowledge' of the human psyche, with the idea that some groups or classes are good for society and others are bad. The revolutionary regime perfects the good, eliminates the bad. Ideology replaced religion as the justification for inter-group cruelty. This elaborate rationale for the things that tyrants have always done has, in the twentieth century, coincided with an enormous growth in the size and power of the state.

Today many despots are found in the so-called Third World.

This chapter draws heavily on conversations with Lord Bauer, Prem Shankar Jha and David Friedman.[2]

They preside over appalling impoverishment, and use the language of Marx to blame the West for their plight. Countries with a colonial past, like Britain, are taught to feel guilty about the 'exploitation' of their colonies.

In East Europe, class theory led to revolution; in the West it led to guilt, the obscure psychological burden which our class carries. The guilt of the West is the inescapable guilt of those who have ended up on the wrong side in the morality play of history.

Compassion is more useful than guilt. It is other directed and rational. Compassion sees a problem and wants to do something. Guilt is messy, obscure, self-centred. Compassion tells us that in the nineteenth century territories were seized by force, people dispossessed, tribal lands aggregated into administrative units that included many races and cultures. It tells us that some lands were well administered, others were not. (We look at part of that record in a moment.) But the notion that this episode created a permanent bloc of disadvantaged countries, like the notion that the white man's burden is now an inescapable burden of guilt, is absurd.

The 'Third World' is a term whose meaning is quite extraordinarily vague. Are the skyscrapers and eight-lane highways of São Paulo part of the Third World? Are we talking about the inhabitants of Mexico City or Monterey, or of the pre-Columbian Indians who still live in remote parts of Mexico? Are we to include the financial districts of Singapore or Hong Kong? It is a term of 'imprecise aggregation'. The broad distinguishing characteristic of those countries which we call Third World is that they receive aid.[3] The concept of 'non-alignment' – giving us the three blocs of the capitalist, the communist and the non-aligned worlds – was launched at the Afro-Asian Conference held at Bandung in Indonesia in April 1955. Among the stars of Bandung were Pandit Nehru of India, President Sukarno of Indonesia and Kwame Nkrumah, who was to become the Prime Minister of Ghana in 1957.

There is now a wide consensus in the West that aid is a

'central component' of world development. (The phrase is that of a vice-president of the World Bank, uttered in 1981.)[4] This line of analysis argues that many countries face a huge structural disadvantage which is partly a product of a history of exploitation, partly a product of their economic weakness. Some Western intellectuals think that transfers to the Third World will have to continue well into the next century in order to enable the less developed countries to catch up.

The presumption that one group of countries should need aid to develop is a questionable one. Western countries did not need aid to develop. Nor did the various parts of the Third World which developed before aid transfers were invented. Is there some presumption of inferiority here? Is this a group of countries who cannot develop on their own, without transfers of aid or donations from us? We feel superior and condescending as we beat our breasts: there are some consolations for our guilt.

The word 'aid' fogs our perspective. Who can be against 'aid'? The very word, associated with diffuse and unspecific guilt, pre-empts criticism, obscures issues, prejudges results. It demands axiomatic approval: being against it is like being against motherhood. But the particular mechanisms of development aid deserve proper attention. We should assess implications, compare results.

Most 'development aid' does not go directly to the pitiful figures we see on television. Development aid is not famine relief, to which the following argument does not apply. The bulk of aid is in the form of government-to-government wealth transfers designed to help lower the cost of financing new projects (because aid comes cheaper than borrowing). But Professor Lord Bauer argues that if development aid goes to rulers on the basis of the poverty of their subjects, it creates a perverse incentive; for it could be argued that government-to-government aid directly rewards policies of impoverishment. If a ruler's policies make people poorer, he can ask for more aid.

The purpose of government-to-government aid is to lower

the cost of the investible resources needed to build a steel mill or drive a road into waste areas. Yet the idea that investment resources are the key to the progress of nations has been a pervasive but false post-war assumption. If it is true, how do we explain the rise of nations from poverty to prosperity in the first place? And how do penniless immigrants, spreading through the world from China or India, rise to wealth? How did indigent Jews establish themselves in a generation? They did not begin with 'investible resources'. The economic history of the world shows that such resources are not a critical factor in material progress. The remarkable success of particular groups of immigrants, which we have charted in previous chapters, suggests a different view of the way the world works. It suggests that men and women who know how to make good use of investment resources are more important than the resources themselves. Investment capital is the result of economic development, not its precondition.

In Africa, during the colonial period, there were Levantine and Asian traders willing to lend to trustworthy African customers. Governments today who wish to invest in major projects can have easy access to funds, though at higher rates of interest than aid. Government-to-government aid helps at the margin. Unfortunately, that does not compensate for its downside effects. Aid also finances bad, excessive government. Aid's political effects have, at worst, been a disaster, empowering late versions of the despotic utopias that ruined the civilised life of Europe in the first half of our century. At best, they have promoted centralised, bureaucratic forms of government.

Government-to-government aid has led to the politicisation of life in newly independent countries. That is in keeping with our times, and would have happened without foreign aid. Nevertheless, foreign aid helps to divert resources from the economic to the political arena. In many countries, the question of who administers and shares in the benefits of government – money, contracts, favours – is the main preoccupation of educated people and a matter of life and death for some.

'We talk about Africa being free,' says Lord Bauer, 'but the poor, wretched individual Africans are certainly less free than they were under the colonial regime. In this terminology, the term freedom is identified with sovereignty, with national sovereignty. But people are certainly not free when they are subject to coercive collectivisation, wholesale expropriation, forced movement from one place to another.'

Centralised government, encouraged by statist ideas from the West, has been disastrous for many multi-cultural, multi-ethnic countries of the Third World. It has led to societies in which all differences are removed except one – that between the rulers and the ruled. It has led to easy seizures of permanent power, acknowledged as dictatorship or dignified by the title of a 'one-party state', where key decisions are made by cadres of officers or Western-educated 'progressive' intellectuals who are the apologists of these Third World courts. The legacy of colonialism was countries that might contain dozens of languages and ethnic groups. The collision between the statism of the new rulers and the living variety of the ruled has led to horrors like the Nigerian Civil War, which began with the secession of Biafra in 1967.

If anything is clear about that imprecise aggregation called the Third World, it is that the poorest and most backward countries are those that have had least contact with the West. 'Throughout the third world the level of material achievement descends,' says Lord Bauer, 'diminishing as we move away from the impact of western contact. Therefore the idea that contact with the west has impoverished them is not only untrue. It's the opposite of the truth.' Some of the poorest places were never colonies at all – Sikkim, Bhutan, Nepal, Tibet, Afghanistan. In Africa poverty-stricken Ethiopia was colonised for only seven short years of Italian rule. The most prosperous Third World country, Hong Kong, is one of the few *remaining* British colonies. If we look to the other pole of the axis of supposed exploitation, we find that some of the most prosperous countries of the world – USA, Canada, Australia, Switzerland – have never had colonies or were once colonies themselves. The old imperialist, Britain, is a relative economic failure. The notion of colonial exploitation – used as a working hypothesis and applied to our world – predicts very little reality.

Lord Bauer, on whose work this analysis draws deeply, constructs a very different picture of the British Empire from the one that now appears in our textbooks.[5] He acknowledges that 'unsavoury things' happened in the earliest days of colonisation. But, from the end of the nineteenth century to the 1930s, there was a great and general improvement in the lives of the inhabitants of the colonies. Before colonisation, the great cities of northern Nigeria had been slave cities. By the 1930s they had become centres of the groundnut trade. The British colonies in Africa and South-east Asia raised living standards and transformed the lives of the local population. 'If one had had to strike the balance for British colonialism in 1930,' says Lord Bauer, 'I would be overwhelmingly favourable. Asked to do the same thing in 1960, I wouldn't be so sure.' What went wrong?

In the 1930s, 1940s and 1950s extensive centralised economic controls were imposed on many colonies in the form of state export monopolies, import licensing boards and state trading companies. A detailed look at what happened in British West Africa reveals how a ready-made framework for totalitarian rule was handed over to the incoming administrations. The traditional centres of power were undermined and the peasant farmer was impoverished. This process was well underway before the British left. Indeed, the British started it.

Until the 1930s, British colonial administrations had envisaged that their successors would be found in modernised native authorities. During the 1930s, however, colonial administration in London fell into new hands. The new men had extravagant notions of what central direction could achieve and were impressed with Soviet-type planning.

Here is novelist Joyce Cary, reminiscing on his life in the colonial service in Nigeria in the earlier part of this century: 'It was the rule then in the Nigerian Service, and has always been one of the guiding principles of British colonial policy, to preserve local law and custom as far as possible, and to do nothing that might break the continuity of local government. Tribal chiefs and tribal councils were to be maintained.'[6] British colonial government was accepted relatively easily because it followed these principles. Consequently, government was straightforward and inexpensive, though not inactive. Public security was maintained. Slave-trading and inter-tribal warfare were suppressed. Monetary and fiscal systems were put under control. Basic education, some public health, and transport were provided. This helped promote the production of cash crops for export throughout West Africa.

In British West Africa there were no European plantations. The large areas which were put under cocoa, palm kernels, groundnuts, cotton and kola nuts were owned and operated by Africans. Capital came from European trading firms or from direct investment by Africans themselves. The consumer goods provided by the traders in return for their cash crops were an incentive to further production. Between the 1880s and the 1930s conditions were transformed through the emergence and spread of these crops. Africans showed themselves well able to think and plan ahead. Millions of African peasants tended and sustained cocoa trees that took six years to mature, even though they did not know what the crop was to be used for. In a few decades the illiterate peasantry of West Africa, and of South-east Asia, planted millions of acres. This involved voluntary changes in their conduct and the sacrifice of leisure. Such enterprise and risk-taking show that the new colonies were, just like every other place in the world, a potential reservoir of entrepreneurial skills. Recent studies of parts of pre-colonial Africa reveal that economic skills were well developed before the colonialists came.

Between the 1930s and the 1950s this beneficent process was reversed. The idea of a gradual political evolution on African lines was replaced by a plan to introduce Westminster style democracy and universal suffrage before independence. The prospective heirs of British rule were no longer the traditional rulers, but the lucky articulate few who had had a Western education at Oxford or Cambridge or the London School of Economics. Limited government intervention was replaced by detailed central economic controls.

The new elite obtained their education at a time when the belief in the efficacy of state action for the solution of economic problems was gaining ground rapidly in Britain. By the 1930s, these ideas were strongly held by a group of influential civil servants at the Colonial Office. These men were unsympathetic to small-scale economic activities like peasant farming. Their ideas were also attractive, for different reasons, to politicians such as Arthur Creech Jones, a Fabian socialist, and Oliver Lyttelton (later Lord Chandos), a dirigiste Conservative, two of the more active Secretaries of State.

A full state monopoly of exports came to West Africa during the Second World War, when the British government announced that it would buy all the cocoa offered for sale. This legitimised the power of buying cartels. The best-known, the Cocoa Buying Agreement, had sparked off a serious producers' strike in 1937. These cartels, in which leading companies brought export products in line with percentage shares agreed among themselves, were bitterly opposed by farmers. But when the Colonial Office established the West Africa Produce Control Board, it gave itself even more extensive monopoly powers. The justification was that this stabilised producer prices.

The beneficiaries of these controlling bodies were, first, the civil servants. The boards extended the power of ambitious bureaucrats and helped many to secure honours. Then, the boards served the interests of cartel members, big companies like the United Africa Company, a subsidiary of the Anglo-Dutch giant, Unilever, and big merchants who acquired for themselves lucrative positions in the export trade, safe from competition. A secondary cycle of politicisation followed. It was alleged that the United Africa Company had excessive market power, which in turn brought demands for more state control. The tempo of political life quickened, bringing the new men into play. In Ghana a major row about import licences in the late 1940s brought to prominence an activist newspaper editor called Kwame Nkrumah. When he came to power, Ghana was the richest black state in Africa. In power, Nkrumah destroyed all opposition to his personal rule, crushed the constitution and the rule of law and permitted his followers to call him 'The Redeemer'.

The farmers suffered most when the marketing boards were set up. There was an explicit undertaking that the boards would not be used as instruments of taxation. A White Paper in 1946 said there would be 'no question of their making a profit at the expense of the West African cocoa producers'.[7] Nevertheless, the boards did accumulate sizeable surpluses at the expense of the farmers. When complaints were put to colonial administrators like Oliver Lyttelton, then Colonial Secretary, and Sir Andrew Cohen, then head of the African Department at the Colonial Office, they justified the policy by saying that there was no future for the peasant in Africa. In a letter to *The Times* on 20 July 1951 the newspaper's colonial editor supported the persistent underpayment of farmers on the grounds that it prevented the emergence of kulaks in Nigeria.[8] British colonial administrators continued to justify the systematic underpayment of African food producers which has helped to drive Africa down a dry path of indigence and starvation. This indigence could have been avoided by the sustained growth of the entrepreneurial skills and human capital of the peasant farmer.

Pandit Nehru was a typical ruler of the new generation, the 'Bandung Generation', as Paul Johnson calls them. He started adult life as an educated idler, as Brahmin, drifting around the English spas after he had finished his Cambridge education. He came from a wealthy background. His father, who was a barrister, once had occasion to reprimand Nehru for paying no attention to his family, saying: 'I do not think that a man who is capable of starving his own children can be much good to the nation.'[9] He drifted into politics in the wake of Mahatma

Gandhi. 'The last word in aristocratic refinement and culture dedicated to the salvation of the underdog', simpered Beatrice Webb, after meeting Nehru.[10]

A new generation of professional politicians took over, all at once, not only in the British Empire but in the French Empire and the Dutch Empire and the Belgian Empire too. All kinds of traditional arrangements, religious powers, powers of tribal chiefs in Africa, powers of princes in India, were suddenly replaced by the new men. They did not opt for constitutions on the American model. Asian and African nationalists had usually worked through parties so that the agitation for independence was concentrated on a particular group. They found it easy to create urban mass parties with a monopoly of the clamour for independence. They tended to look to the Soviet model of a single party even when their states were given multi-party constitutions. The idea of global exploitation came naturally to the new men.

The constitution which India adopted at independence was a model one – a liberal document. (But then the Soviet Union has a liberal constitution, apart from the clause that allows the Party to do anything it believes to be in the public interest.) In India's case, its weakness was the clutch of directive principles, adopted as an appendix to the constitution, which enabled the government to control the economy as closely as it wished. The government has been the Congress Party, which, though riven with dissent, has been in power for all but two and a half years since independence. Its ideology is vaguely socialist and anti-communist. It is committed, above anything else, to retaining and strengthening its power.

The country Nehru inherited was vast and disparate, the second largest in the world. Its population was greater than the total population of the Western hemisphere, with an annual increase greater than the population of Britain or France. There were scores of different major languages, and at least fifteen different major scripts. Five-sixths of the population lived in some 600,000 villages, most of them unconnected to roads. The only common language was English, but the government has not designated English as an official language, seeing it as part of the colonial inheritance.

As a country, it is as unsuitable a candidate for detailed economic planning as could be envisaged. Any government would have had its hands full maintaining law and order, improving education and communication, maintaining good relations with its difficult neighbours. Nehru had difficulty uniting the country. He had to send troops into Goa to ensure their accession to the Union; Kashmir had to be subdued. There was the constant threat of communal violence between Muslim and Hindu. With these problems to contend with, Nehru and his government set out to pull India's people out of poverty, and towards equality. The method chosen was the 'five-year plan' – adopted from the Soviet Union, and used in many other developing countries. The plan was a mixture of nationalism, Fabianism and Stalinism.

The government did not attempt the wholesale appropriation of the private sector. It was content with a mixed economy in which the public sector was to dominate, the private sector to be subservient. This commutation for the private sector was fortunate, because the private sector in India has produced remarkable successes, increasing the wealth of its people. Most agricultural land is still in private hands. India feeds itself and exports grain. Government and the public sector continue to impoverish the country.

Today India is trying to evolve away from its own late version of the 'British disease'. Its main problem is the slow-moving legacy of a planning system developed by post-war planners using licensing and investment restraints to further 'social' objectives and speed development. The planners felt they must ration access to foreign exchange. They wanted to avoid duplication in the system. They gave preference to Indian industries. To avoid excessive concentrations of industrial power, they supported small to medium-size companies and curtailed large ones. The restraints and the rationing would, it was argued, allow capital movement into huge projects in which private industry could not invest because the gestation periods were long and the sums colossal.

The five-year plans proposed levels and areas of public investment, selected industrial sectors in the private sector that were to be encouraged and set overall targets for growth. The system of licensing was so complex and detailed as to be farcical. A licence had to be obtained to start a business, to move into a new product area, to export and to import. The government was involved in all major wage negotiations. It even had to approve some salaries offered to individuals in senior positions in private companies. The anti-monopoly legislation prevented any one company from supplying more than 30 per cent of the market for a product. In a poor country, with a small market for many goods, that percentage is easily reached. While India was proclaiming to the world its need to expand production, exports and wealth, it was actually fining companies for producing 'too much' – more, that is, than their licence specified.

The series of unintended consequences that sprang from this system of close licensing is both tragic and comic. The system was meant to curb the growth of powerful large companies, and encourage the new small company. It did the opposite. It was meant to give the government control over everything produced in the country. It failed. It was supposed to prevent the emergence of a class of conspicuously wealthy industrialists. It did the opposite.

The system, weighed down with the inefficiency of the public sector, has retarded the potential growth of the country and the wealth of its people. It is difficult to put figures on this failure, but some experts argue that the gross domestic product of the country could have been 25–30 per cent higher today than it is.[11]

Out of 200 major enterprises in the public sector, more than 190 are making losses, many of them substantial. These enterprises have been built by expropriating private savings and by continually raising duties and taxes. They continue to drain more and more money out of the Indian economy into the pockets of inefficient managements and swollen bureaucracies. The current five-year plan envisages the appropriation of some 40 per cent of potential savings and bank deposits for further investment in the public sector. The long-term effects compound. Monopolies of essential services, like the power supply industry, have not only been run inefficiently, but have found it impossible to maintain consistent supplies, making life for industrial users constantly uncertain. Energy is overpriced, constituting another tax. Yet many industrialists are unconcerned. They are the beneficiaries of licensed monopoly. They pass on high costs to the customer, secure in the knowledge that nobody can undercut them.

Politicians continue to make excuses for the public sector. George Fernandes, a socialist and former Minister for Industry, points to the National Textile Corporation which runs 117 mills, employs 150,000 workers and produces 25 per cent of the country's textiles. It is a hospital for private sector casualties. Instead of allowing a mill to close the government has invariably stepped in and taken it over. Fernandes puts this down to 'failure' in the private sector.

Fernandes claims that industrialists have no complaints. Successful ones may, indeed, have reasons to like the system. But newspapers are full of letters and articles about the high prices, inefficiency, tangled bureaucracy. India's public sector displays characteristics no different from public sector enterprise throughout the world. The Indian government has entered many different areas of industry; it has spread its limited expertise thinly. Its ministers and bureaucrats cannot be in several hundred places at once. No government can possibly possess enough information to make the decisions about price, supply, demand that running industries demands. India's economy suffers from a massive information deficit that comes from the lack of competition and the lack of signals from market prices.

It is an economy of shortage. Everything falls short of the demand. Expansion and growth are braked. Consider steel. In 1968 the privately owned Tata Steel lodged the first of its applications to raise its capacity from 2 million tonnes to 4 million tonnes, in the process replacing equipment installed in 1922. At the same time the government planned to build a 4 million tonne plant in east India – an area designated as underdeveloped. Tata then offered to raise their capacity to 6 million tonnes, meeting the target set for the two plants. Their planned cost, raised from their own funds, and from the stock market, was half that of the government project. They were refused permission. The government claimed 'social objectives' in deciding the location of the steel plant, which normally means that political promises have been made. All the main supposed objectives of planning, the conserving of capital and resources, the setting of targets for growth fade beside the political objectives of retaining power, accommodating political pressure, placating a marginal constituency. The other argument, that the state has to develop heavy industries because the private sector cannot raise the investment resources, and cannot stand the long lead times, is revealed as nothing but a ploy.

In the private sector, too, every product is under-produced, the inevitable result of a licensing system. A licence to produce may take three or four years to negotiate. Even if products go to the market as quickly as possible, the level of production licensed four or five years earlier is invariably out of date. One company recently announced a new scooter. It is already taking advance deposits from people willing to put their money away for six to eight years, at no interest, in order to be on the waiting list to buy the scooter.

The licensing system has created a class of featherbedded, wealthy industrialists, old-fashioned plutocrats, quite opposed to opening up the economy to genuine competition. These privileged licence-carriers stay close to the politicians and the bureaucracy, keeping themselves in favour with political donations and the other forms of corruption necessary to ensure a steady flow of licences. If they run up against the monopoly legislation they have other options. The first is to enter the black economy. Measured as a percentage of

India's gross national product, the black economy is one of the largest in the world. Every day, in the Jharen Bazaar in Bombay, millions of pounds' worth of goods are traded – raw materials, polyester, cloth, grain, diamonds, gold. It is done quite openly, and it is all entirely illegal. Yet it is the lifeblood of Bombay, providing many jobs and incomes. It also makes the few rich industrialists still richer. What they produce beyond their licensed capacity, they sell on the black market. Many unlicensed companies operate entirely through the black market. For years, industrialists have sent money secretly out of the country to lie idle in Swiss bank accounts. Under a rational system, that money could have stayed in India, put to productive use. Wherever competition is limited by government control, the rich get perks and the poor stay poor.

Another course for the Indian industrialist is to go into entirely new fields of production. Consequently, a common part of the Indian scene is the large diversified company, producing everything from bicycles to fertilisers. It is a recipe for high prices and inefficiency. As long as it can get its licence, a company does not need to have expertise in producing the new product. Economies of scale are lost. Monopoly, shortage and high taxes mean high prices and bad products.

The inefficiency of India's private sector is compounded by the network of political control that exists outside the licensing system. Many large plants were sited in what are now cities or built-up areas. It would make economic sense to sell the valuable land and reopen the plant in a less developed area – perhaps even one designated as underdeveloped. The trade unions, which are strong in India, fight against the closure, unwilling to accept transitional job losses even though substantial redundancy payments are offered. Sometimes the state, using laws passed at trade union insistence, may take half the profit on the land sale, or even appropriate the land for its use at a non-negotiable price. The result is that old plants stay where they are. The inefficiencies are maintained.

Wherever Indians go, abroad, they succeed – in Africa, in

Britain and in Hong Kong, where exports, per head of population, are forty times as high as India's. Indian nationals control some 20 per cent of the Hong Kong economy. At home these talents are suppressed. A Planning Minister said at independence that industrialists could not be trusted to act in the national interest. They had to be told. The administrative attitude to entrepreneurs, according to Prem Shankar Jha, an Indian journalist, is one of 'public contempt and private graft'. His explanation for this is that the Brahmin class who took over government retained the traditional attitudes of feudal landowners. They had always treated the trading classes, a lowly group with no access to land, as marauders, a rogue class with domicile. Consequently the trading classes owed no loyalty to anyone but clansmen. This major social conflict has yet to work itself out.

Today India is struggling out of this mindset. Licensing laws have been relaxed. We went to the new Maruti car plant where something quite unprecedented is going on. Maruti produce a low-cost car assembled from parts sent by Suzuki in Japan. The product is bang up to date and its fuel economy is good. It is also selling a lot more than expected, a supply-side success which has shown that there is a consumer market for a low-cost modern car in India. As the car rapidly took 75 per cent of the market, the planners' vision of the Indian market was once again shown to have been wrong.

The new manager of Maruti admits he has not much to compete with. The other car plants still make cars to designs licensed from British Leyland in the early fifties. There had been no incentive to change them. Maruti no longer have to buy headlamps from five separate manufacturers because of monopoly rules. Auto-parts have been 'de-licensed'. Prime Minister Gandhi has spurred competition by pruning the system of production licences and he is trying to get away from corruption-inducing quotas.

At the beginning of the 1980s India was standing low down on the world poverty scale. The average income of her 676 million people was £120 a year. In the same year the average income of an Egyptian was £220, of a Nigerian £420, of a Portuguese £1120 and of a Swiss £6780. Something needed to be done, and the Gandhi measures are an attempt to do it. They are already producing results. In 1985 limits on private investment were lifted and companies raised $3.8 billion of private capital, up from $2 billion in 1984. Despite lower tax rates, tax revenue has been rising.[12] But such a policy has difficulties. Exports are slow because the prices of Indian products are too high, their quality too low. Indian producers of capital goods have lost out too because their factories are overmanned. Businessmen do not like competition. Bureaucrats do not like to lose power and corrupt perks from licensing.

By stopping short of communism and wholesale nationalisation, by making some public investments of lasting value, India is a healthier and wealthier place than it might have been. Yet the struggle to capitalise on its successes and to release the creative and entrepreneurial skills of its people is proving a tough one. Socialist reaction allied with licensed industrial greed makes a powerful combination. One generation of businessmen have learned to survive in the political market. They will hold tenaciously to their positions.

Change is tricky. The unexpected is always waiting in the wings. But Rajiv Gandhi is riding on a wave of liberalisation that is travelling all over the world. It is applying a healthy and invigorating pressure, and reminding us of something we should have realised earlier. There are not three worlds. There are just lots of places, facing the same problems. The 'Third World' is not different. It too is trying to solve the economic problem. The economic problem is intensely tough – dangerous, obscure, intractable. It demands huge personal effort. Government requires incredible personal skills even when we limit its scope. The detail of Britain's and India's problems may be different, but we are after the same thing. We are all trying to avoid poverty, and poverty, as Alfred Marshall said, is the cause 'of the degradation of a large part of mankind'.[13] Poverty keeps coming from a new direction. It is out there waiting. We have to keep studying. It creeps up. There is poverty in Cambuslang and Calcutta and Uttar Pradesh. It is the main threat to our freedom and it degrades people everywhere.

History is a black book of cruelty and error. Some evil people have planned evil outcomes. Successful societies deny them power. Most unfortunate outcomes are the unintended consequences of the acts of men and women who were trying to do the right thing, by their own lights or in the estimation of their betters. We Europeans may regret mistakes made by our elders, but they are not our mistakes. The settlement of white farmers in parts of Africa led to unhappy outcomes. The authoritarian regime of South Africa is a tragedy. The handover of power in many colonial countries was inept. We may well regret that so much power was given away by people who were under the spell of an intellectual error. All we can do now is let compassion prompt the rational use of our limited knowledge.

'I would like to see governments', says Lord Bauer,

> attend to their traditional functions, the most important of which is public security, that is the security of personal and legitimate property. I would like to see governments which perform these tasks and at the same time refrain from close economic controls over their societies. And I particularly emphasize external commercial contacts, which are not just channels of goods and services, but of new ideas, new methods, new attitudes which a population can accept or not accept as they wish.

There is a modest utopian tradition in the New Enlightenment.[14] It goes like this. Suppose there was perfect mobility in the world, and states had no authority to keep anyone from moving to other states. Then the citizens of one state would consist of just as many people as wish to live under that one particular jurisdiction. The constitution of each state would represent the ideals of the founders and the rules that citizens were expected to follow. There might be strict Salt

Lake City states and anything-goes San Francisco states, communist states and capitalist states, small ones and large ones. States would shrink and expand like firms adjusting to their income, as unpopular states lose citizens and popular ones gain them. New states are always being born; old ones are reforming themselves, as people come up with new ideas; and old states are dying. Though this 'framework for utopia' follows other utopian traditions in its search for a perfect way to live it does not define what that way should be, a much more inspiring notion than the end-of-history static society of socialist utopian thought.

Some people take fantasy one stage further and imagine a time, some centuries hence, when we will have learned to construct space stations and anchor these new habitats at the so-called Lagrangian Points in the earth–moon system (where a body placed in a stable orbit will remain forever), or even further off in the asteroid belt. The space stations will be huge spoked wheels which recreate gravity by spinning and creating a centrifugal pressure on the inside of the rim.[15] The economist David Friedman says he got the idea for a perfect 'anarcho-capitalist' society from Robert Heinlein's book *The Moon is a Harsh Mistress*.[16] If Heinlein could imagine it, who could say it was not possible, in a space habitat where you were free to start a new society without any limiting conditions? 'We need more separate spaces to accommodate our diverse and various needs,' says Friedman.

The left has lost its enthusiasm for the future. Its science fiction shows us sterile or retrogressive societies and police states with multiple varieties of uniforms. Milton Friedman, David Friedman's father, points out that the policies of the 1928 Manifesto of the Socialist Party of America have mostly been enacted into law. He goes through the points one by one, showing that the once radical demands have nearly all been achieved.[17]

Is it possible to write an alternative liberal or libertarian manifesto? The New Enlightenment is more optimistic, but highly provisional. Its thoughts about the future, like its framework for utopia, will be more an aspiration than a prediction. New Enlightenment authors have been reluctant to guess what the twenty-first century may be like if socialism withers. Our future tense is conditional.

We become ever more mobile. People with skills or talents or capital are free to roam the world. They settle in those places which are most convivial, drawing in like-minded experts or enthusiasts. These fledgling international communities are sometimes called science parks. Boulder, Colorado, or Cambridge, England, or Palo Alto, California, or Perth, Australia, or Geneva, Switzerland – these are not metropolitan centres like New York, London or Sydney. But they offer cultural and physical climates which appeal to people with a lot of human capital. From these specialised talent clusters, industries grow. To retain their human capital resources some nation states will have to change their policies. Socialist states have tried to match these communities by setting up academic towns with lavish privileges.

A more modest effect of the transnational mobility of the future are the wider horizons which living abroad will offer. The explosion of holidays and time-sharing contracts, aided by instant interpretation devices, will have a liberating effect. People with more modest credit or skills will be able to offer their labour on an international market, causing states to work hard to make their cities and fiscal regimes attractive to people who bring prosperity and diversity. Perhaps we will learn, once and for all, that nearly all movement between countries brings economic benefits. Ordinary people will take their savings and open a bar in Spain, start a building company in Portugal, buy a vineyard in Bordeaux.

In this possible future world, the internationalisation of video, broadcasting and computer networking, the use of satellites as a means of communication, will enable us to leap frontiers, rendering socialist efforts to corral information and manipulate the culture of ordinary people as pointless as it was odious. The rethinking of welfare benefits not only livens up labour markets but re-establishes the sensible, responsible habit of paternity. The rate of divorce moderates. Without rewards for the one-parent family, the pattern of childbearing alters.

The old practice of sending children to an institution called a school looks odd in the twenty-first century. Parents with purchasing power in the form of vouchers or tax credits choose teachers, and visit educational agencies much as we visit travel agencies today, choosing a package of courses for the term or the year. Experience is more enlightening than formal education; so children travel abroad to study foreign languages. Commercial companies teach dexterity with information technologies, perhaps in exchange for part-time labour.

Employers may take over the role of teaching skills and technology, communicating their most up-to-date knowledge to the up-and-coming generation. Most parents still want their children to acquire basic skills. But the artificially long childhood and adolescence imposed by state regulation in the interest of the education profession has been identified as a dreadful error. A 'liberal education' is exposed as a sham, dreamed up during the nineteenth century by administrators afraid of the popular franchise. Children move into industry-based schools, just like the ones who want to learn dancing or music today.

Much business will be conducted from home, as digital networks and telecommunication links overcome geography and distance. The middle classes will continue to flee cities until the incompetence and corruption of local authorities leads to the widespread contracting-out of municipal services. Surplus land and unworked buildings will be sold off or bulldozed to create parks and open spaces. Landscape contracting becomes big business in the early twenty-first century. Traffic congestion is partially solved by new road-metering devices that use electric pulses to impose proper costs on urban travel by car, a system already in use in Hong Kong. The deregulation of urban buses and taxis works the biggest transformation. The removal of controls rapidly evolves the hybrid taxi–omnibus. Larger vehicles serve a hub and spoke network. Comfortable vans run passengers to their specific destinations.

The Japanese experience, of the last thirty years of the twentieth century, in privatising security and police work district by district, is eventually copied elsewhere. The Japanese achieved continuous falls in urban crime for thirty years before municipal and state police forces in other nations were thrown open to competitive bidding. It took a long time for the obvious success of the Japanese experiment to sink in. Politicians, over-attentive to middle-class pressure groups and the police lobby, took a long time to realise how bad their police were at keeping order in the poorer parts of communities where crime is the biggest enemy of progress.

Another professional group whose dignity is savaged by the tide of deregulation are doctors and para-medics, such as nurses and ambulance crews. The rebirth of private health insurance in the wake of the decay of the state services creates entirely new expectations about the quality of medical care. The promise of preventive medicine suddenly comes true, not just because individuals expect it, but because insurance underwriters insist on regular check-ups and health maintenance contracts. The monitoring of health is almost entirely automated by interactive diagnostic machines, in agencies on High Street or Main Street. Databases provide medical information. The old GP, mainly replaced by health centres offering a clutch of medical specialisations, is still valued for his intuitive skills and knowledge of the family.

Exercise habits which had been fashionable under state health care, give way to swimming, which some health maintenance contracts insist on. It is the dissolution of the state electricity utility monopolies that makes everyone swimmers. With electricity costs at a quarter of their previous level, neighbourhood swimming pools grow as rapidly as parks. In Britain, the privatisation of energy suppliers such as British Gas and the Central Electricity Generating Board has had effects that were completely unforeseen. The old utility monopolists are compelled to share their grid networks. At both ends of the wires or mains, there is a competitive market in energy supply and energy-using appliances. The giant coal, oil and nuclear stations have been beaten in price by small private contractors using hydro and wind power. To everyone's surprise the auctioning off of the British National Coal Board has generated new worker-owned pits so productive that they have kept open mines which experts had agreed were uneconomic.

As agriculture ceases to be a highly protected mercantilist folly, the patterns of world food cultivation alter to reflect real comparative advantage. The flatlands of the Ukraine match the US and Canadian prairies as Soviet citizens are allowed to own land again. Livestock prospers in most locations but Argentina and Australia again become prime suppliers to world markets. Fruits and vegetables return to where soil and climate rather than subsidy have placed them. The most surprising of the new food sources are the continental shelves. The enclosure of the near seas leads to a much more efficient husbanding of marine resources. The establishment of property rights on the moon disappointed the initial enthusiasm of the contractors. They had wanted to plough back the huge profits from their orbiting space stations. Except for some limited mineral ore recovery, a modest tourist traffic and penal use, the moon has proved useless and valueless.

Just as children become active agents in the labour and trading markets, so compulsory retirement gives way to individual choice. Most older people prefer to stay in work but to alter its intensity. Their pension rights are not drawn from the state social insurance funds. The only state role is now to insist that people make minimal provision for their old age. Beyond that they are free to choose any mix of pension and annuity contracts.

As the redemption of the education vouchers of the citizens of richer nations becomes a significant earner for the once-named 'Third World', so poorer communities begin to attract such welfare recipients as remain. Instead of living in Easterhouse or some other dismal municipal tract in a depressed area, the welfare recipients find their limited money goes so much further in Tunisia or Senegal. Such transfers of wealth divert more money than ever the formal 'aid' programmes ever did. The re-creation of stable currencies lost since the collapse of the gold standard after the First World War was the biggest advance stumbled upon. Prior to 1914 all the state currencies were held to their gold values, so that the world really shared a common currency. This was the reason for the great growth of international trade in the nineteenth century. Paradoxically it was the final relaxation of state monopolies that allowed private banks to issue currencies that got us away from inflation-prone, government-printed notes.

The world is a better place. There is a severe curtailment of the powers of governments and administrative salariats. Many different kinds of constitutions emerge. All the most successful spell out basic laws clearly, define the executive's role narrowly, design institutions to defend constitutional rights and limit the discretionary power of elected politicians. They tell government to do only those tasks that governments need to do. Socialism has lost its freehold on the future.

The world is information-rich. Information is transmitted widely and fast, not just through integrated digital networks but, more importantly, via mobile people and an open price system. Human knowledge remains imperfect and fallible. Humans know it. Where this sense of our ignorance prevails, there is hope. We are players in the adventure game of the future, whose ending we cannot begin to guess. Who could possibly know what treasures, what monsters, are waiting?

And will there be peace or war in the twenty-first century? We cannot say or guess. Socialism promised peace, but gave us poverty and tryanny. We *can* say that no true version of the liberal idea sanctions physical aggression except in defence of the rights of the individual and the rule of just laws.

*

Back to the present. Ideas do not rule the world. *People* with ideas do that, even when a new idea is progressing by stealth, in many different places. Even the best ideas are surrounded by the darkness in which unintended consequences wait. Our time has been led by some bad ideas. Entranced with ideas, we have behaved as if the idea was everything, as if intentions were results, as if a blueprint was a reality. In our time clever people have pushed ideas right through to their moment of truth. Never mind the human consequences.

The liberal idea is a good idea, but clever people are not enough. There is nothing inevitable about the success of this idea. It needs excellent defenders, tough, articulate, trained men and women, loaded with human capital. For that matter, there is nothing inevitable about history. Different people, different skills in different places, might have changed the outcome of the Russian Revolution or amended the Treaty of Versailles.

We have written this book from the perspective of the individual. The individual is not absolutely free. I am not free to walk across Wales, because there are mountains in the way. That reminds me that the real world is contoured. We exercise our freedoms within the limits of those contours. When we modify those contours, we extend our freedom and our choice. The creation of wealth is a partial victory over natural limits. It builds a pass over the mountains, starts a high valley road, takes us where we had not been before.

There is a double magic about the liberal idea. Not only does it free us to live as we choose within the real limits or contours that bound our lives. It also releases the human energy and knowledge that pushes back those limits, better than any other idea we know. Who can say no to it?

Notes

1 *The Death of Socialism*

1 Paul Johnson is the author of *A History of the Modern World* (Weidenfeld & Nicolson, 1983); John Grey is a Fellow of Jesus College, Oxford, and author of *Hayek On Liberty* (Basil Blackwell, 1984); Martin Anderson is a Senior Fellow of the Hoover Institution, Stanford University, California, and policy adviser to President Ronald Reagan; Lord (Ralph) Harris of High Cross is the General Director of the Institute of Economic Affairs, London; Antony Fisher is the President of the Atlas Economic Research Foundation; Milton Friedman is a Senior Fellow of the Hoover Institution, and a Nobel laureate: F. A. Hayek was awarded a Nobel Memorial Prize in Economics in 1974.

2 Kenneth Minogue is Professor of Political Science at the London School of Economics. He is author of *Alien Powers: The Pure Theory of Ideology* (Weidenfeld & Nicolson, 1985).

3 Thomas Kuhn is the author of *The Structure of Scientific Revolutions* (University of Chicago Press, Chicago, 1970).

4 Quotation from an interview for *The New Enlightenment*. Subsequent references marked *TNE*. Not all New Enlightenment thinkers share Hayek's optimism. Milton Friedman, for example, points out that 'periods of freedom are very rare in the history of the world. The natural state of mankind is tyranny and misery. . . . Those of us who believe in a free society must always keep in mind that there must be basic forces working against our ideas. It may be that a free society is an unstable equilibrium position that cannot be maintained.'

5 Bernard Mandeville, *The Fable of the Bees* (Pelican Classics, 1970). For F. A. Hayek's views on Mandeville, see *Dr. Bernard Mandeville*, Proceedings of the British Academy, vol. LII (1966). See also Kenneth Minogue, *Alien Powers*, pp. 13–14.

6 *The Wealth of Nations* (1776), Book IV, ch. 2.

7 *Conjectures and Refutations* (Routledge & Kegan Paul, 1972). For this story, see pp. 34–6.

8 Quoted in *ibid.*, p. 153.

9 *A History of the Modern World*, ch. 1.

10 William H. Beveridge's *Report on Social Insurance and Allied Services* was submitted to His Majesty's Government in November 1942. See also *Full Employment in a Free Society* (Allen & Unwin, 1944).

11 Lionel Trilling, *The Liberal Imagination* (Harcourt Brace, New York, 1979).

12 This letter is quoted in R. F. Harrod, *The Life of John Maynard Keynes* (Pelican Books, 1972), pp. 514–15. The full quotation on 'moderate planning' is: 'Moderate planning will be safe if those carrying it out are rightly orientated in their own minds and hearts to the moral issue.'

13 F. A. Hayek, *The Road to Serfdom* (Routledge, 1944), p. 10.

14 Sonia Orwell and Ian Angus (eds), *The Collected Essays, Journalism and Letters of George Orwell*, vol. 3 (Penguin Books, 1970), p. 143.

15 *The Road to Serfdom*, p. 106.

16 R. Max Hartwell, 'The Re-emergence of Liberalism? The Role of the Mont Pelerin Society', unpublished article, p. 1.

17 R. Max Hartwell, 'Concerned Liberals: The Founding of the Mont Pelerin Society', unpublished article, p. 10.

18 Theodore H. White, *America in Search of Itself: The Making of the President 1956–1980* (Jonathan Cape, 1983), p. 108.

2 *Serfdom Today*

1 John Stone and Stephen Mennell (eds), *Alexis de Tocqueville On Democracy, Revolution and Science* (University of Chicago Press, 1980), p. 375 (from *Democracy in America*, pt 2, bk 4, ch. 6).

2 Sir Reginald Murley is past President of the Royal College of Surgeons; David G. Green is the author of *Working-Class Patients and the Medical Establishment* (Gower/Maurice Temple Smith, 1985); John C. Goodman is the author of *The Regulation of Medical Care: Is The Price Too High?* (Cato Institute, 1980); James Buchanan is Director of the Center for Study of Public Choice at George Mason University,

Fairfax, Virginia; Charles Murray is the author of *Losing Ground: American Social Policy 1950–1980* (Basic Books, New York, 1984).

3 The case of Mr William Benton was researched for *TNE* by Jeremy Bristow.

4 The Pharisee's second prayer is: 'Thank God I am not a woman.'

5 Pedro Schwartz is Professor of Economics at Instituto de Economia de Mercado, Madrid, and a member of the Mont Pelerin Society.

6 The independent Griffiths Report into the management of the NHS was led by Roy Griffiths, Managing Director, J. Sainsbury PLC.

7 In a Gallup Poll, taken in March 1985, doctors rate highest for 'honesty and ethical standards'. Their 75 per cent rating was followed by the police at 55 per cent, lawyers at 46 per cent, and university teachers at 38 per cent. Such findings are common. See Robert Nozick, *Anarchy, State, and Utopia* (Basil Blackwell, 1975), pp. 232–5, for an interesting discussion on doctors' goals.

8 David G. Green pursues his research into health economics at the Institute of Economic Affairs, London. Material in this chapter also draws on the work of Ralph Harris and Arthur Seldon, in particular their book *Over-ruled On Welfare* (Institute of Economic Affairs, 1979). For David Green's work, see also *Which Doctor?* (Institute of Economic Affairs, 1985).

9 The National Center for Policy Analysis in Dallas, Texas, was founded by Antony Fisher and John C. Goodman in 1983.

10 Examples of the work of the public-choice school is available in Britain in Gordon Tullock, *The Vote Motive* (Institute of Economic Affairs, 1976) and *The Economics of Politics* (Institute of Economic Affairs, 1978).

11 Anne Kreuger, 'The Welfare Costs of Tariffs, Monopolies, and Theft', *Western Economic Journal*, 1967.

12 Keith Middlemas, *Politics in Industrial Society* (André Deutsch, 1979).

13 In conversation with David Graham in 1981.

14 For a critical account of the idea of a 'new class' see Peter Steinfels, *The Neoconservatives* (Simon & Schuster, New York, 1979).

15 See note 2 above.

3 *Human Capital*

1 Gary Becker is Professor of Economics at the University of Chicago and the author of *The Economic Approach to Human Behavior* (Chicago University Press, 1977); Anne Wortham is the author of *The Other Side of Racism* (Ohio State University Press, 1981); Walter Williams is Professor of Economics at George Mason University, Fairfax, Virginia, and the author of *The State Against Blacks* (McGraw Hill, New York, 1984); Ed Snider is the owner of the Philadelphia Flyers ice hockey team; Tibor Machan is a Senior Fellow at the Reason Foundation, Santa Monica, California; Irving Kristol is Editor of *The Public Interest*.

2 Gary Becker, *Human Capital* (National Bureau of Economic Research, New York, 1964).

3 George Gilder, *Wealth and Poverty* (Basic Books, New York, 1981), p. 70.

4 Charles Murray, *Losing Ground: American Social Policy 1950–1980* (Basic Books, New York, 1984), pp. 156–64 and 176–7.

5 Quoted in Thomas Sowell, *The Economics and Politics of Race* (William Morrow, New York, 1983), p. 38. See also his *Knowledge and Decisions* (Basic Books, New York, 1980) for a brilliant account of the advantages of economic over political choices.

6 *Ibid.*, pp. 120–32.

7 *Ibid.*, pp. 246–7.

8 *Wealth and Poverty*, p. 151.

9 Robert Nozick, *Anarchy, State, and Utopia* (Basil Blackwell, 1975), p. 163.

10 *Ibid.*, pp. 160–4.

11 See Roland Barthes, *Mythologies* (Paladin, 1973), pp. 15–25, for a rather different interpretation.

12 Quoted in Jane Feuer, Paul Kew and Tise Vahimagi, *MTM: Quality Television* (BFI, 1984).

13 J. A. Schumpeter, *Capitalism, Socialism and Democracy* (Allen & Unwin, 1974). Originally published in Great Britain in 1943.

4 *Making It*

1 Akio Morita is co-founder (together with Masaru Ibuka) and Chairman of Sony; Sir Peter Thompson is Chairman and Chief Executive of the National Freight Consortium; Israel Kirzner is Professor of Economics at New York University; George Heilmeier is Senior Vice-President and Chief Technical Officer of Texas Instruments, Dallas, Texas; Antonio Martino is Professor of Monetary History and Policy at the University of Rome; George Gilder is author of *Wealth and Poverty* (Basic Books, New York, 1981) and *The Spirit of Enterprise* (Viking, 1985).

2 For our account of the success of the Japanese economy we rely heavily on Gilder, *The Spirit of Enterprise*, chs 7 and 9.

3 Keith Marsden, 'Links between Taxes and Economic Growth: Some Empirical Evidence', *World Banks Staff Working Papers*, No. 605, 1983. The following excerpt may be of interest: 'Overall, an increase of 1 percentage point in the total tax/GDP ratio is estimated to decrease the rate of economic growth by 0.36 percentage points,' *ibid.*, p. 30.

4 Thomas J. Peters and Robert H. Waterman, *In Search of Excellence* (Harper & Row, New York, 1982).

5 *Ibid.*, p. 159.

6 *Ibid.*, p. 245.

7 *Ibid.*, p. 171.

8 *The Spirit of Enterprise*, ch. 7.

9 *Ibid.*, p. 132.

10 *Ibid.*, p. 135.

11 *Newsweek*, 30 June 1986, p. 23.

12 In conversation with *TNE*. See also Antonio Martino, 'Another Italian Economic Miracle' and 'Measuring Italy's Underground Economy', *Policy Review*, 1980.

13 Our account of 'Austrian' economics draws upon Geoffrey Sampson, *An End to Allegiance* (Temple Smith, 1984), ch. 6.

14 *The Spirit of Enterprise*, p. 145.

15 Antonio Gramsci, *Selections from Prison Notebooks* (Lawrence & Wishart, 1973), p. 34.

16 John Maynard Keynes, *The General Theory of Employment, Interest and Money* (Macmillan, 1976), p. 221.

17 *The Spirit of Enterprise*, p. 93.

18 A. David Silver, *The Entrepreneurial Life* (John Wiley, New York, 1983).

19 *The Spirit of Enterprise*, pp. 93–4.

5 *A Constitution for Liberty*

1 Richard Epstein is Professor of Law at the University of Chicago and the author of *Takings: Private Property and the Power of Eminent Domain* (Harvard University Press, 1985); Oliver Letwin is a former policy adviser at 10 Downing Street; Norman Barry is Professor of Politics at the University of Buckingham; Kurt Furgler is a former President of the Swiss Confederation and now head of the Department of Public Economy; Claude Massy is the Liberal MP for Vaud, Switzerland; A. E. Dick Howard is Professor of Law and Public Policy at the University of Virginia, Charlottesville, Virginia.

2 Adapted from Robert Nozick, *Anarchy, State, and Utopia* (Basil Blackwell, 1974), ch. 10.

3 Gottfried Dietze's work includes *Magna Carta and Property* (University of Virginia Press, 1965), *The Federalist* (Johns Hopkins Press, 1960), and *America's Political Dilemma* (Johns Hopkins Press, 1968).

4 John Locke, *Two Treatises of Government* (1690), Second Treatise, section 4.

5 *Ibid.*, section 7.

6 *Ibid.*, section 8.

7 *Ibid.*, section 6.

8 *Ibid.*, section 222.

9 See note 1 above.

10 Richard Epstein in conversation with *TNE*.

6 *Private Worlds*

1 Paul Johnson, *A History of the Modern World* (Weidenfeld & Nicolson, 1983).

2 Lord (P. T.) Bauer is Emeritus Professor of Economics at the London School of Economics; Prem Shankar Jha is Deputy Editor of the *Times of India*; David Friedman is the author of *The Machinery of Freedom: Guide to a Radical Capitalism* (Arlington House, New York, 1978).

3 Lord Bauer in conversation with *TNE*.

4 Quoted in P. T. Bauer, *Reality and Rhetoric: Studies in the Economics of Development* (Weidenfeld & Nicolson, 1984), p. 38.

5 See note 1 above, and also P. T. Bauer, *Equality, the Third World and Economic Delusion* (Weidenfeld & Nicolson, 1981).

6 Quoted in *Reality and Rhetoric*, p. 91. From Joyce Cary, *Selected Essays*, 1976.

7 Quoted in *Reality and Rhetoric*, p. 172.

8 *Ibid*.

9 Quoted in Paul Johnson, *A History of the Modern World*, p. 472.

10 *Ibid.*, p. 473.

11 Prem Shankar Jha in conversation with *TNE*.

12 *The Economist*, 28 June 1986, pp. 13–14.

13 Quoted in John Maynard Keynes, *Collected Writings*, Vol. 10 (Macmillan, 1972), p. 170.

14 Robert Nozick, *Anarchy, State, and Utopia* (Basil Blackwell, 1974), pp. 297–334.

15 This design is associated with Dr Gerard K. O'Neill and known as the 'O'Neill Colony'.

16 Robert Heinlein, *The Moon is a Harsh Mistress* (New English Library, 1969).

17 Milton and Rose Friedman, *Free to Choose* (Penguin Books, 1980), pp. 360–1.

Bibliography

Anderson, Martin, *The Federal Bulldozer* (MIT Press, Cambridge, Mass., 1964).

Barry, Norman, et al., *Hayek's Serfdom Revisited* (Institute of Economic Affairs, London, 1984).

Bauer, P. T., *Equality, the Third World and Economic Delusion* (Weidenfeld & Nicolson, London, 1981).

Reality and Rhetoric: Studies in the Economics of Development (Weidenfeld & Nicolson, London, 1984).

Becker, Gary, *The Economic Approach to Human Behavior* (Chicago University Press, Chicago, 1977).

Wealth and Poverty (Basic Books, New York, 1981).

Buchanan, James M., et al., *The Economics of Politics* (Institute of Economic Affairs, London, 1978).

Buchanan, James, et al., *The Consequences of Mr Keynes* (Institute of Economic Affairs, London, 1978).

The Limits of Liberty: between Anarchy and Leviathan (University of Chicago Press, Chicago, 1975).

Butler, Eamonn, *Hayek: His Contribution to the Political & Economic Thought of Our Time* (Temple Smith, London, 1983).

Epstein, Richard A., *Takings* (Harvard University Press, Cambridge, Mass., 1985).

Friedman, David, *The Machinery of Freedom* (Arlington House, New York, 1973).

Friedman, David D., *Price Theory* (South-Western, Cincinnati, 1986).

Friedman, Milton, *Capitalism and Freedom* (University of Chicago Press, Chicago, 1962).

Friedman, Milton & Rose, *Free to Choose* (Penguin Books, London, 1980).

Gilder, George, *The Spirit of Enterprise* (Viking, London, 1985).

Wealth and Poverty (Basic Books, New York, 1981).

Goodman, John C., *The Regulation of Medical Care: Is The Price Too High?* (Cato Institute, San Francisco, 1980).

Green, David G., *Working-Class Patients and the Medical Establishment* (Gower/Maurice Temple Smith, London, 1985).

Grey, John, *Hayek On Liberty* (Basil Blackwell, Oxford, 1984).

Harris, Ralph, and Seldon, Arthur, *Over-Ruled On Welfare* (Institute of Economic Affairs, London, 1979).

Hayek, F. A., *The Road To Serfdom* (George Routledge, London, 1944).

The Constitution of Liberty (Routledge & Kegan Paul, 1960).

Law, Legislation and Liberty (Routledge & Kegan Paul, London, 1982).

Knowledge, Evolution and Society (Adam Smith Institute, London, 1983).

Johnson, Paul, *The Recovery of Freedom* (Basil Blackwell, Oxford, 1980).

A History of the Modern World (Weidenfeld & Nicolson, London, 1983).

A History of the English People (Weidenfeld & Nicolson, London, 1985).

Kirzner, Israel M., *Discovery and the Capitalist Process* (The University of Chicago Press, Chicago and London, 1985).

Locke, John, *Two Treatises of Government* (J. M. Dent, London, 1924).

Macfarlane, Alan, *The Origins of English Individualism* (Basil Blackwell, Oxford, 1978).

Mandeville, Bernard (ed. Harth, Phillip) *The Fable of the Bees* (Penguin Books, London, 1970).
Middlemas, Keith, *Politics in Industrial Society* (André Deutsch, London, 1979).
Minogue, Kenneth, *Alien Powers: The Pure Theory of Ideology* (Weidenfeld & Nicolson, London, 1985).
Murray, Charles, *Losing Ground: American Social Policy 1950–1980* (Basic Books, New York, 1984).
Nozick, Robert, *Anarchy, State, and Utopia* (Basil Blackwell, Oxford, 1975).
Ortega y Gasset, Jose, *The Revolt of the Masses* (W. W. Norton & Co., New York and London, 1932).
Peters, Thomas J., and Waterman Jr., Robert H., *In Search of Excellence* (Harper & Row, New York, 1982).
Popper, Karl R., *Conjectures and Refutations* (Routledge & Kegan Paul, London, 1963).
Rawls, John, *A Theory of Justice* (Oxford University Press, Oxford, 1972).
Sampson, Geoffrey, *An End To Allegiance* (Temple Smith, London, 1984).
Schumpeter, J. A., *Capitalism, Socialism and Democracy* (Unwin University Books, London, 1943).
Smith, Adam (ed. Raphael, D. D., and Macfie, A. L.) *The Theory of Moral Sentiments* (Clarendon Press, Oxford, 1976).
Smith, Adam (ed. Skinner, Andrew) *The Wealth of Nations* (Penguin Books, London, 1970).
Sowell, Thomas, *Knowledge and Decisions* (Basic Books, New York, 1980).
The Economics and Politics of Race (William Morrow & Company, New York, 1983).
Steinfels, Peter, *The Neoconservatives* (Simon & Schuster, New York, 1979).
Stone, John, and Mennell, Stephen (eds.) *Alexis De Tocqueville on Democracy, Revolution, and Society* (University of Chicago Press, Chicago, 1980).
Tullock, Gordon, *The Economics of Politics* (Institute of Economic Affairs, London, 1978).
The Vote Motive (Institute of Economic Affairs, 1976).
Wanniski, Jude, *The Way the World Works* (Basic Books, New York, 1978).
Williams, Walter E., *The State Against Blacks* (McGraw-Hill, New York, 1976).
Wortham, Anne, *The Other Side of Racism* (Ohio State University Press, Columbus, 1981).

Index